THE ORVIS STREAMSIDE GUIDE TO
Leaders, Knots, and Tippets

TOM ROSENBAUER

Illustrations by Rod Walinchus
Photographs by Tom Rosenbauer

Lyons Press

Text and photographs copyright © 2000 by Tom Rosenbauer
Illustrations copyright © 2000 by Rod Walinchus

Printed in China
10 9 8 7 6 5 4 3 2 1

Design by Compset, Inc.

Library of Congress Cataloging-in-Publication Data

Rosenbauer, Tom.
    The Orvis streamside guide to leaders, knots, and tippets / Tom
Rosenbauer; illustrated by Rod Walinchus.
        p.   cm
    ISBN 1-55821-984-6 (hc.)
    1. Leaders (Fishing) 2. Fishing knots. 3. Tippets (Fishing) I. Title.

SH452.9.L43 R67 1999
688.7'9124—dc21   99-045681

CONTENTS

FOREWORD

As far as I know, there are no books available today
that cover leaders, tippets, and knots in a concise for-
mat, written from a novice's perspective. I tried to
write the book I would have wanted 30 years ago,
when even the thought of removing a leader from its
package gave me the jitters. The few references out
there that cover leaders, including my own *Orvis Fly-
Fishing Guide*, are outdated and contain no mention of
braided leaders, poly leaders, or fluorocarbon tippet.
There are some great choices in leaders and tippets,
but apart from catalog copy there is no written refer-
ence on how to make these choices.

The importance of choosing the proper leader is un-
derestimated both in casting and in presentation. You
can be using a superb fly rod and a brand new fly line,
but if your leader is not properly tapered, the whole
outfit can feel sluggish. A difference in tippet diameter
of .001" or a couple of feet of tippet material can mean
the difference between a frustrating day and a fun and
productive one. In my experience as a fly-fishing in-
structor I found basic leader and tippet design to be
harder for students to grasp than the double-haul. And
even experienced fly fishers disregard the importance
of the right leader. When switching rods with friends, I
am often amazed at the state of their leaders.

The knots you see in this guide might be tied differ-
ently than the way you've been taught. I have written

these instructions as clearly as I could, assuming you have never tied one of these knots before. These directions may not be the same as the ones you see in other books, because these are the way guides and other experienced fly fishers tie them.

Some of your favorite knots might be missing. In my opinion, and the opinion of highly technical fly fishers like Jim Lepage, head of fly-fishing product development for Orvis, knots like the Improved Clinch Knot and Turle Knot are best treated as fly-fishing history.

My only goal in writing this book was to make your days on the water easier and more fun. We don't always need to catch fish to have a good day, but broken leaders and lost fish are never positive experiences.

ACKNOWLEDGMENTS

The fly-fishing business is a close-knit community. There is often a fine line between colleagues, friends, fishing buddies, guides, editors, and publishers. Rather than trying to figure out where the following people fit in, I would like to thank them in alphabetical order for the great things they've taught me about lines, leaders, and tippets, and writing over the years: Rick Alden, Tony Biski, Jay Cassell, Frank Catino, Joe Dion, John Harder, Steve Huff, Jim Lepage, Nick Lyons, Tony Lyons, Dave Perkins, Perk Perkins, Rick Ruoff, Tom Shubat, Tony Stetzko, Rod Walinchus.

Chapter 1

SETTING UP YOUR OUTFIT

You've watched for the UPS delivery truck every day and finally it arrives, with one long skinny box and one square package: your new fly rod outfit! You open the rod box and all is as expected, but when you open the box that contains the reel, line, and backing—surprise! Instead of the neatly wound reel you saw in the catalog, you're faced with an empty reel, a large spool of fly line, and a smaller spool with 100 yards of backing. The leader isn't attached; it's coiled up in a small plastic bag. And you thought you were going fishing this afternoon.

You can avoid this dilemma by purchasing your gear from a reputable fly shop or mail order operation: They'll set up your outfit, making all the essential connections and providing you with a reel that is loaded and ready to go. (If they won't or can't do it, take your business elsewhere.) All you need to tell them is whether you reel with your left or right hand; make sure you specify *which hand you use to crank* to avoid any confusion.

Unless you intend to fish with a personal guide at your side every minute, or are prepared to throw leaders away after they get too short, you'll need to learn how to maintain your terminal tackle, as this line/leader/tippet arrangement is called. And you'll have to learn at least a couple of those dreaded knots. However, anyone capable of lacing a pair of shoes or knotting a tie can deal with terminal tackle.

Maybe you forgot to ask someone to set up your outfit, or you didn't know any better. Or perhaps you already owned a reel and just bought some new fly line or backing. Find a quiet, well-lighted place with plenty of room and no small children or cats present. Turn on some music and plan for an hour of interrupted fun. If you need reading glasses or have even a remote inkling that you might, make sure they are handy.

I'll assume you know whether you will be cranking with your right or left hand. (By the way, there is no single correct way to do this, no matter what your Uncle Gus, who has been fly fishing for 50 years, tells you.) Some right-handed casters prefer to crank with their right hands, so they switch the rod to their left hand when reeling in a fish. I do because I am so strongly right handed that I have trouble doing anything with my left hand. Many right-handed casters set their reels up so they can crank with their left hand and don't have to switch. It's your choice.

Make sure the drag on the reel is set up properly, as most reels can be switched from right- to left-hand retrieve without tools or with a small screwdriver at most. It matters because you want to be able to tighten the drag on the line-out direction when a fish is running, but you want a smooth, easy-spinning reel on the line-in direction. Refer to the owner's manual for your reel to figure out how this is done.

Attaching the Backing

Find the end of the backing and attach it to the reel with an Arbor Knot, which allows you to start spinning the reel while the backing snugs up against it. Now start winding the backing onto the reel, making sure that it's going in the right direction. The backing should be wound on uniformly tight, and you should guide it from one side to the other as you wind, so it goes on the spool evenly. It helps to have someone hold the backing spool on a pencil and keep tension on it. You can put the spool of backing in a box to prevent it from rolling all over the room. Run the backing through a heavy book placed between the box and your reel to keep some tension on it.

When you get to the end of the backing, you will probably have to attach the line. Sometimes line and

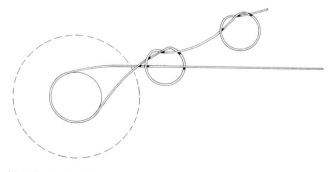

Attaching the backing with an Arbor Knot.

backing combinations come to you factory-spliced with epoxy, but most times they will be in two separate packages. For this operation you need to learn the Nail Knot, and you will need either a six-inch piece of backing (just cut it off the end of your backing), a narrow-diameter tube, or a stir stick. There are also tools specifically made to tie Nail Knots. Nail Knots are not only used to tie backing, but also to tie a leader to the opposite end of the fly line. Since it is much easier to tie a Nail Knot in backing than in springy monofilament, this is a good place to learn it.

Find the back end of the fly line, which will invariably be labeled with a sticker that says, "This end to reel," or "This end to backing." If you can't find the sticker, the back end will usually be the end that comes off the spool easiest. Still having trouble finding the end? If you have a double-taper line (labeled somewhere on the package as DT*F, where * is a number from 1 to 12), both ends are the same and it doesn't matter. If you have a weight-forward line (marked WF*F), it does matter. Feel the line and you'll notice that one end tapers quickly to a thicker section and the other end is uniformly thin for more than 20 feet. This thin end gets knotted to your backing.

Attaching the Line

The Nail Knot is a simple concept that can be fiendish to execute, especially if you want the result to look neat. All you have to do is wrap the backing or leader material over itself and then bring the tag end back un-

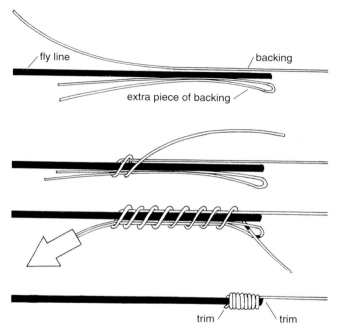

fly line

backing

extra piece of backing

trim trim

The Nail Knot can be tied in four steps (top to bottom).

derneath the wraps. It's difficult to pass the tag end back under the wraps while keeping them snug, and most people use a loop of material or a tube to pass the end back under the wraps.

Lay 2 feet of fly line on the table in a straight line, with the end of the line in front of you. Fold the piece of backing in half and lay it alongside the fly line, with the closed end even with the end of the line (if you are using a tube or stir stick, lay it alongside the line). Pull a foot of backing off the reel to give yourself some working room, then pinch the backing up against the fly line and extra loop of backing (or tube), with the standing part of the backing (the part that goes to the reel) pointing toward the end of the line and the tag end of the backing toward the rest of the fly line. Start the Nail Knot about 2 inches from the end of the line. You can afford to cut a little off the end of the line, which gives you some insurance in case the Nail Knot slips as you tighten it.

Wind the backing back over itself, over the line, and over the tube or extra loop, toward the end of the fly line. I like to make about seven or eight turns when knotting backing to fly line. After you've completed these turns, pass the tag end of the backing through the extra loop of backing and gently pull the piece of backing from the other end so it pulls the tag end of the backing back under the wraps. If you are using a tube, just pass the tag end of the backing through the tube until it sticks out the other end. Once you have passed the backing under the turns, either remove the tube or the extra piece of backing. The trick here is to keep pinching the wraps so they stay in line and close to the fly line; if the wraps jump over themselves, the resulting knot might be strong but it won't be neat, and it might get hung up passing through the guides.

The nasty part is tightening the knot. Gently pull on the tag end of the backing while still pinching the wraps to keep them in place. Pull gently on the standing part of the backing—don't touch the fly line yet. Pull on the tag end again. Pull on the standing part again. Keep repeating the process until you have a neat, barrel-shaped knot and the wraps are as tight at one end as they are on the other. Next grab the tag end with a pair of pliers and pull it tightly against the standing part of the backing. Then wrap the fly line around one forefinger and the standing part of the backing around the other and pull them against each other. This is the way stress will be applied when you are fishing and it is your test to see how well you've done the Nail Knot. If your knot is properly tied and tightened, it will dig into the line when pulled instead of slipping off the end of the line. Now trim the tag ends of the fly line and backing very close to the knot with a pair of sharp scissors. (Don't use monofilament snips, which will fray the backing instead of cutting it neatly.)

For the ultimate in a smooth connection, coat the knot with a *thin* application of flexible waterproof cement such as Pliobond, Barge Cement, or even Super Glue. Don't worry if you are tying the knot at streamside or if you don't have any glue handy: I find that the Nail Knot is so smooth and secure that cement is not essential.

Now wind the fly line with tight, even turns, as you did with the backing. It won't take as long as winding the backing, but it can be tricky because fly lines are mounted on plastic spools that often come apart in the middle of the winding operation, resulting in a tangled mess. Wind slowly and make sure the spool halves are pressed together securely. You may want to put a pencil or other thin object through the hole in the spool. It really helps to have someone hold the spool while you wind.

If the spool falls apart and the line gets tangled, take a deep breath. Slowly untangle the line, walk around the room as you untangle it, or take the whole mess outside so you don't end up with a tight pile of line that will only need to be untangled all over again.

Chapter 2

ATTACHING THE LEADER

There is a confusing array of methods that can be used to connect a leader to a fly line. The connection can be as simple and as permanent as tying a knotless leader directly to the fly line with a Nail Knot. Most anglers opt for some type of permanent loop at the end of the fly line, which lets you switch from one kind of leader to another with a simple loop-to-loop connection. Loops are either made from braided nylon or solid monofilament, which can be either a nylon co-polymer or PVDF, often called fluorocarbon. (PVDF is a plastic packaging material first used for fishing line

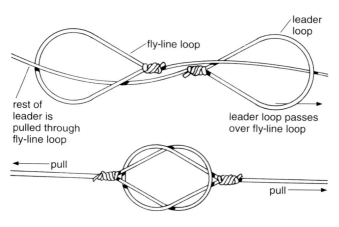

Attaching the leader to the fly line with a loop-to-loop connection.

in the mid-1990s; I'll talk about its properties shortly). You must remember that both braided and solid leaders can be attached to a fly line with a braided loop, but only solid nylon leaders can be attached to a solid loop.

Knotting the Leader Directly to the Fly Line

This connection simply ties the butt or heavy end of the leader to the end of the fly line with a Nail Knot. If the leader came packaged with a loop at one end, simply cut it off. It's the cleanest of connections but also the least versatile: Eventually you will need to replace

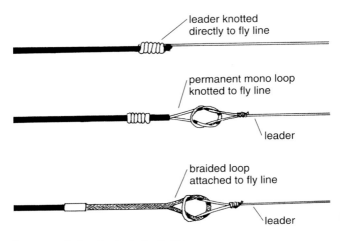

Three ways to tie a leader to the fly line.

the leader, which will require cutting off a small piece of the end of the fly line and tying on a new leader with another Nail Knot.

Most anglers consider tying a Nail Knot on a par with a visit to the dentist or paying their income taxes. However, if you use knotted leaders or if you start with a knotless leader and then rebuild it numerous times during the season, you can typically get through an entire season without having to remove it and replace it with a new leader. This method works best for anglers who fish the same types of conditions all season long—for instance, someone who fishes only long leaders on ponds or who fishes only dry flies in small streams.

Tying a Nail Knot in Solid Monofilament

The name of this knot comes from the fact that a nail was used to provide rigidity to the line while the knot was tied, even though a tube makes it easier to pass the coils back under themselves. This is not as easy as doing it with backing. Backing is soft, flexible, and, well, friendly. Heavy monofilament is wiry, inflexible, and seems to squirm in every direction except the one you want it to. For this knot I would definitely suggest a tube.

There are many tools on the market designed to help you tie a Nail Knot. Models go in and out of fashion; if you feel you need help with a knot that practice won't fix, try one. Rather than dating myself and suggesting a particular model, I'll tell you that any knot-tying tool sold in the Orvis catalog has been thoroughly tested. Don't expect a miracle. I've found that people who begin using a tool from day one are adept with it, but if you have been tying Barrel Knots for 30 years and finally decide you need some help, it will be like trying to learn the knot from scratch.

I'd recommend a five-turn knot for tying monofilament up to about .023″ to your fly line; for anything heavier, three turns will suffice. Don't try to use more than five: the knot will be almost impossible to tighten and it won't be any stronger.

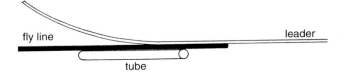

1. It helps to make sure the end of your fly line and the monofilament are as straight as you can get them. Stretch both in your hands. Place the tube parallel to the fly line, making sure that the open end of the tube (if one end is closed) points toward the end of the fly line. Lay the piece of monofilament alongside both the line and the tube. The long part of the leader (the part that will not be trimmed) should be coming off the end of the line, and about 10 inches of tag end should run up along the fly line.

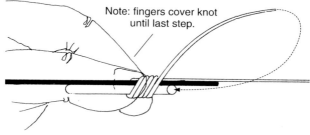

Note: fingers cover knot
until last step.

2. About an inch from the end of the fly line, pinch the monofilament against the line and begin winding the tag end back over itself, over the fly line, and over the tube. The wraps must progress toward the end of the fly line. The hardest part is to take that first wind, because it needs to double over itself in a direction it does not want to travel. Each turn should be tight against the preceding one, with absolutely no gap in between winds. The fifth turn will still be some distance from the end of the line, but that's okay; the knot tends to slip off the end of the line if you get too close. You can cut a full 2 inches off the end of a fly line without hurting its performance in the slightest. Now slide the thumb and forefinger that you have not been using to wind up over the wraps, and keep pinching them!

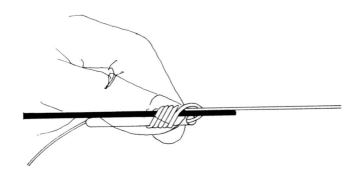

3. Pass the tag end through the tube so that it passes under the turns you just made. You don't have to pass the whole thing under so long as the end of the tag end is now beyond the first wrap. You should still be pinching the five wraps.

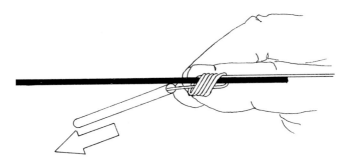

4. Transfer the pinching to the other hand without letting go of the coils. Pull the tube out in a direction opposite the end of the fly line. Withdraw

the tube quickly and keep pinching those five wraps tightly. Don't look at the wraps and do not stop pinching! Have faith.

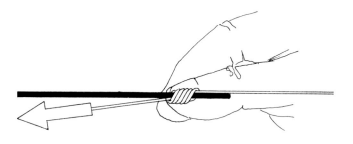

5. Still without taking your fingers off the wraps, pull gently on the tag end until it tightens against the wraps. Switch pinching hands again and pull on the standing end. You may want to repeat this a few times until the turns are snug but not tight up against the fly line. *Now* you can stop pinching and check your coils. If they are not smooth and even, you can try working them back into position at this point with your fingernail. You can even position the knot to move it closer to the end of the fly line now if you wish. If things look too bad, slip the mono off the end of the line and start over.

6. Once you are satisfied with your coils, pull tightly on both ends of the monofilament. It helps to wrap the butt of the leader around your hand and hold the tag end with a pair of pliers.

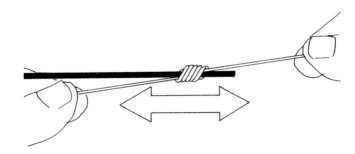

7. Finally, pull on the fly line and the standing part of the leader with nearly as much force as you can with your hands. This snugs the knot completely and tests the knot before you put it into action. Trim the tag end of the leader and the end of the fly line as close to the knot as you can.

Some anglers tie a variation of this knot called the Needle Knot, where the end of the leader is shaved to a fine sliver with a single-edge razor blade and inserted about ¼ inch into the end of the fly line. A Nail Knot is then tied at the point where the leader re-emerges. This knot offers a very smooth connection and comes out of the tiptop (guide at the tip of the rod) easily because the leader comes out of the center of the fly line.

Some people coat their Nail Knots with Pliobond, Barge Cement, or similar waterproof flexible cements. They argue that it smoothes out the knot. I don't like doing this because it adds a little weight and bulk to the knot, and seems to make the fly line hit the water harder.

Speed Nail Knot

This is an easier way to tie a Nail Knot, especially if you are just attaching a short piece of monofilament for a permanent loop. You also don't have to find a tube: the only tool you need is a stiff piece of smooth metal like a nail or straightened paper clip. This knot is fairly tricky with a long leader, and cannot be used if there are any knots in your leader.

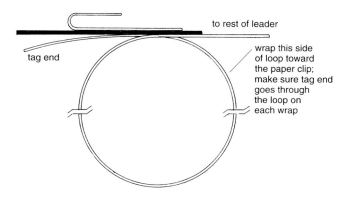

to rest of leader

tag end

wrap this side of loop toward the paper clip; make sure tag end goes through the loop on each wrap

1. Lay the paper clip (or nail) alongside the fly line close to the end. Place about 6 inches of the tag end of the monofilament (the butt section if you are using an entire knotless leader—and don't forget to cut off the loop) alongside the line and clip. This part should point away from the end of the line.

17

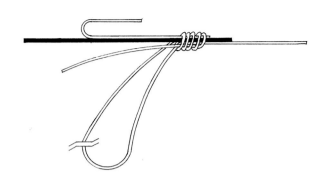

2. Make a big loop with the rest of the leader. The fine end of the leader should come off the tip of the fly line. Wind the end of the loop nearest the end of the line away from the end of the line five times. Wind over the clip, the fly line, and the leader itself. When winding this loop, you must clear the end of the leader for each revolution, so the standing part of the loop must be pretty short. If you're attaching a 15-foot leader, the loop you wind will be over 7 feet long and nearly impossible to control. That's why I recommend using this knot for attaching a short piece of butt material to a fly line, or at most a short leader like the butt section of a saltwater leader.

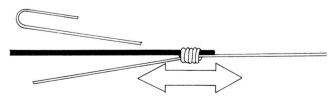

3. Pull on the standing part of the leader (the piece coming off the end of the fly line) until the loop is pulled snug to the fly line. You may have to remove twists in the loop as you do this. When the knot is snug against the clip and the line, slip the clip out from under the coils and tighten the rest of the knot as you would a standard Nail Knot.

Solid Monofilament Permanent Loop

Here, a 3- to 6-inch piece of monofilament equal to the diameter of the butt of a leader (usually .021″ to .029″, or even heavier with saltwater lines) is tied to the fly line with a Nail Knot while a Perfection Loop is tied on the other end of the monofilament. This method lets you change from a 7½-foot leader in small streams to a 15-footer on a still pool in a matter of seconds. With a simple loop-to-loop connection, you don't have to tie a knot. The disadvantage of this connection is that it is slightly bulkier and might catch on weeds, but once some pressure is put on the loops they collapse and keep a fairly slim profile. Another disadvantage is that this kind of loop is too stiff to use with the more supple braided leaders.

Braided Loops

This is the loop used by most anglers today (page 21). It's strong, flexible, and versatile because it can be used with either solid or braided leaders. Best of all, you can stick one onto your fly line without having to tie the dreaded Nail Knot. Orvis fly lines come with braided loops factory-installed, or you can buy kits to do them yourself. Braided loops don't hold onto a fly line with a knot; instead, they grip the line with coils similar to the paper finger cuffs kids play with. The end opposite the loop is hollow; a piece of tight flexible tubing over the end of the braid keeps it from slipping off when no pressure is applied to the loop. It also keeps the braid from fraying. For further security, factory-installed braided loops are glued to the line.

Sometimes you hear about these loops slipping off a fly line. When investigating these failures, invariably I find that someone has carelessly reeled the leader inside the rod guides and then yanked on the loop connection when it caught on a guide. If the loop has not been carefully glued to the line and the end covered with tubing, it gets loose when there is no pressure on the loop and it can slip off. This can't happen when a fish is on, because the harder a fish pulls, the tighter the connection becomes.

Attaching Your Own Braided Loops

I like carrying a couple of these loops along with a short piece of nylon tubing in my fishing vest. If I somehow lose the end of my fly line along with my leader connection, I can then put a new loop on the end of my fly line in a couple of minutes without having to tie a Nail Knot. Don't laugh—I've had the end of my fly line burned off by a cigar, cut off by a big fish that took my line too close to a sharp underwater rock, and once I fatally pinched a line in a car door.

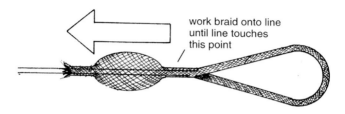

work braid onto line
until line touches
this point

1. First, make sure the braided loop plus the hollow single end is no more than 2 inches long, and that the open end is cut off clean and not frayed. Sometimes braided loops come in the package as long as 4 or 5 inches, which is way too long. When the braided connectors get this long, they add too much mass to the end of your line and can make presentation a little sloppy. If the open end is frayed, cut it cleanly with a pair of scissors. Line snips don't do as good a job on braided material. By the way, if you don't carry a pair of scissors in your fishing vest, you should. Besides doing some jobs on leaders that snips can't do, scissors are needed to manicure flies at stream-side—to turn an Adams into a spent spinner, for example. Some Swiss Army knives have lightly serrated scissors that are perfect.

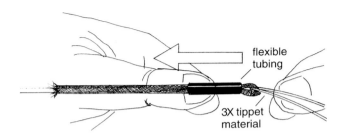

flexible tubing

3X tippet material

2. You should also carry flexible tubing that just barely fits over the end of your fly line. The tubing comes with the braided loops when you buy them. Cut a piece of tubing to ½ inch and put it aside for a moment. Slip the open, hollow end of the braided loop connector onto the end of the fly line, and work the end of the fly line all the way up into the braid until it is snug against the base of the loop. There's usually a spot where the loop has been glued that forms a natural stop. The easiest way to work the line up inside the loop is to inchworm it forward bit by bit. If you don't advance the end of the line all the way to the end of the hollow braid, you'll get a soft spot where your cast will hinge when the leader is uncoiling at the end of a cast.

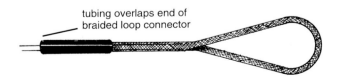

tubing overlaps end of braided loop connector

3. Make sure the end of the line stays put and thread a 7-inch piece of 3X or 4X tippet material through the braided loop. Place the two ends of the tippet material together, then use them to thread the flexible tubing over the loop, onto the fly line, and back to a point where the tubing is centered over the end of the braid. Wrapping the tippet over a finger helps to pull against the tubing. Work slowly and carefully; if the tubing is very tight, wet the braid with some water to lubricate it. If you go too far and the tubing slips beyond the end of the braid (and this happens often), just slip the loop connector off the line, pull off the tubing, and start over.

The tubing will ensure that the loop connector does not slip off when it's not under tension. You don't have to worry about a properly installed loop connector coming off, because the harder the pull on the loop, the tighter the braid digs into the fly line. Although you don't need to use glue at streamside, if you're doing this at home and have the luxury of waiting an hour or so, put a drop of gap-filling cyanoacrylate (Super Glue) over the braid, right where it is covered by the tubing.

Making Your Own Braided Loops

It's easy to make your own braided loops with some hollow braided monofilament and a crochet hook. Start 6 inches from the end of the braid. Make sure that the movable guard on the crochet hook is folded back along its shank, then poke the end of the hook through the braid until it is inside the hollow part. The easy way to do this is to face the hook opposite the end of the braid while working the hook inside the braid, then reverse the hook so it points toward the end of the braid. Push the hook up inside the braid 1 inch, then poke it back outside the braid. Go up 2 inches outside the braid and grab the braid with the end of the hook. At this point fold the movable guard on the hook so that it protects the point of the hook. Pull the hook back through the braid, pulling the end of the braid

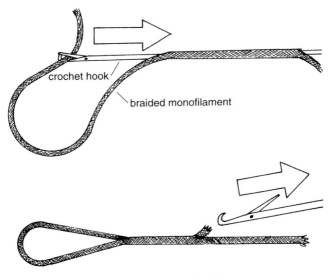

crochet hook

braided monofilament

Making your own braided loop using a crochet hook.

with it. Hold the loop you have formed to make sure it does not get pulled through, and draw the end of the braid back through your original entry point. Once the hook has been pulled through, you can adjust the size of your loop by pulling on the sides to make it bigger or by pulling on the tag end to make it smaller. Once you are satisfied with the size of your loop, cut the tag end close to the point where it exits from the braid and apply a few drops of high-viscosity Super Glue or Zap-A-Gap.

Chapter 3

PICKING THE RIGHT LEADER

Most people have no trouble accepting the fact that a leader removes the fly from the vicinity of the heavy, opaque fly line, which can spook a fish or at the very least make it suspicious. We usually want the fly line to land at least 6 or 7 feet away from the fly, and thus the suspected lie of a fish, so leaders must be tapered in some way. Why? Because a 6-foot level piece of 4X tippet tied to a size 12 dry fly will land in a big pile after the cast is completed. As we'll see shortly, this big pile is not always unwelcome—but not when it lands right next to the fly line!

A well-developed loop at the end of a forward cast is accelerating briskly. A leader that is too stiff and short, without a taper to absorb energy along its length, would slam your fly into the water. Conversely, a leader that is too limber and long will prevent your fly from ever reaching its intended target. Somewhere in between a long thin leader and a short stiff one is a reasonable compromise. All leader tapers incorporate a stiff, heavy butt section (the part that attaches to your fly line) and a midsection that forms a transition between the heavy butt and the fine end where you tie your fly—the tippet. The tippet is usually level and at least 20 inches long. The exact formula varies depending on the materials used to make the leader, but the most common taper is 40 percent butt, 30 percent mid, and 30 percent tippet. The taper can be made by joining sections of level material with many knots, or it can be of one continuous piece of extruded material without a single knot. The taper can even be constructed by making the butt and mid sections of one kind of material and the tippet of another, as in poly and braided leaders.

One final thought on leaders: It is not always enough to drive a fly with precision into a spot the size of a dime 60 feet away. A stiff, tapered leader can do that easily. However, you need a more natural presentation in order to attract fish. Especially in stream fishing, once your fly hits the water it should appear to be unconnected to anything, and the farther your fly is from the stiffer part of the leader (which means a long, flexible tippet), the better. So there is nearly always a delicate balance between accuracy in the air and flexibility on the water. In our eagerness to cast the fly just where we want, the flexibility part is often ignored. I'll show you ways to help.

Types of Leaders

As in many areas of fly fishing, there's a bewildering array of options when the time comes to pick a leader. Don't let it bother you. Fly fishing is a subjective, individualized passion, and although there is a never a right or wrong way to do something, there is usually a simple solution that takes care of 95 percent of the conditions you'll encounter on the water. If you don't want to bother with the intricacies of leader designs, just buy a 9-foot 4X knotless leader with a loop on the butt end (most of them come this way) and be done with it.

knotted leader

knotless leader

Later, I'll show you how to make this one leader fit almost all conditions with a few spools of tippet material and a couple of knots. If you like to fiddle with gear, though, read on . . .

Knotted Leaders

If you want to learn about leader design and practice your knots, I'd recommend that you start by tying your own knotted leaders. Do this and you'll learn how leaders are tapered, you'll learn how to tie a wicked Barrel Knot, and you'll save money in the process. Whether knotted or knotless, pre-made leaders cost about three bucks each. Knotted leaders will cost you less than 50 cents each if you make them yourself.

Tapered leaders: a knotted leader (left) and a knotless leader (right). The stiffer butt section loops onto the fly-line loop; the fine end (tippet) is the flexible part where the fly is tied.

Knotted leaders are made according to formulas like the one below, which specifies the length of each section. You'll notice how the leader tapers down from heavy to light, and that the heavy butt section and tippet section are longer than the transition sections in between. When you sit down to tie your own leaders, you'll need a yardstick (which is easier to use than a tape measure), a pair of snips or sharp scissors, and good light. Tie a Perfection Loop (page 92) in the butt section material, then measure the butt section, adding perhaps an inch for the end of the knot that will be snipped off. Don't worry if any of your sections are an inch or so longer than the formula once you're finished, as leader taper is not that precise a science.

Nine-Foot 4X Orvis Knotted Leader Formula

LENGTH	DIAMETER
36"	.021"
16"	.019"
12"	.017"
6"	.015"
6"	.013"
6"	.011"
6"	.009"
20"	.007"

The Perfection Loop is not the easiest knot to tie, but it is preferred for putting a loop in the heavy butt section because it is neat and compact—an important consideration when you're working with nylon that's .021″ or .023″ in diameter. You can tie a Surgeon's Loop (simply a double or triple overhand loop, as shown on page 95) in the butt of your leader, but in addition to being a bulky knot, the Surgeon's Loop ends up cocked in relation to the rest of the leader. The Perfection Loop always ends up perfectly in line with the leader.

After you've tied a loop in the end of the .021″ section, measure out 29 inches (the 28 inches plus the extra inch you'll cut off). Cut a 16-inch section of .019″ (14 inches plus an inch at either end, since you'll be tying a knot at both ends). Tie a three-turn Barrel Knot (page 86) between the two sections. Now cut the .017″ piece and repeat the process, knotting it to the .019″ piece.

If you look at the formula, you'll notice that no two adjacent sections differ by more than .002″. There are a couple of reasons for this. One is that the transfer of casting energy moves down the leader more smoothly if there are no abrupt changes in diameter. The other is that the Barrel Knot, the neatest and cleanest knot ever developed for nylon, loses strength when you jump more than .002″ between sections. You can make a knotted leader with fewer sections (and knots!) using Surgeon's Knots (page 84), but the resulting leader would not have the delicacy needed for most trout fishing. Bass and saltwater leaders are often made this way because delicacy is not quite so important.

When you're casting, you'll notice that knotted leaders feel different than knotless leaders. Not better, not worse—just different. Some anglers believe that the compound taper you can get with a knotted leader (in other words, not a constant or smooth taper but a heavy butt, then a quick jump to the tippet using short pieces of material) is better than the smoother taper dictated by the machines that extrude and stretch knotless leaders. Others feel that the mass added by the knots helps unfurl the leader at the end of the cast.

It's also easier to modify a knotted leader on the water, at least when you're starting out. If you refer back to that 9-foot 4X leader formula, you'll notice the tippet section (the piece of .006″ nylon) starts at 20 inches. But every time you tie on a new fly—or lose one in the trees—you will lose anywhere from a half-inch to an inch of material between the knot and whatever you trim off. After a half-dozen fly changes, the tippet is now only 14 inches long. At this point it becomes so short that the fly slams into the water. The fly also becomes a less credible imitation in moving water, because the shorter tippet does not allow it to move as freely in the currents. So you need to tie on a new tippet, and with a knotted leader, you know exactly where it goes. With a knotless leader, you can't see exactly where your tippet ends, and unless you carry a micrometer with you (don't laugh—some people do), it's hard to be certain where the new piece goes.

With a knotted leader, you tie a new piece of .006″ tippet material to the 6-inch piece of .007″ material and you're back in business. Eventually, the 6-inch piece of .007″ stuff will also get too short and you'll have to replace that section, too. The intermediate transition sections are really there as connectors, though, so as long as they are long enough to tie a knot in, they're okay. When I tie my own leaders, I always make the last four 6-inch sections about 7 inches long, so I can get more mileage out of them.

Knotted leaders do have drawbacks, however. I think the weight of the knots makes a knotted leader land a touch harder on the water, an important consideration in shallow water where trout are spooky. The knots can also catch on debris such as aquatic weeds, sticks, and cottonwood fluff on the surface. And once the knots are loaded up with even a tiny amount of debris, the leader performs miserably. There is also the strength issue, but it's not as bad as you think. If you assume that a knot between two pieces of material gives you about 90 percent of the breaking strength of the weaker piece, so long as the knots in the heavier material are tied properly, the only link you have to worry about is the knot that joins your tippet to the rest of the leader. Let's say your tippet is 2-pound test, and it's joined to a piece of 3-pound test, which is joined to a piece of 4-pound. The link between your tippet and the first section breaks at about 1.8 pounds (2 $\times$ .9). The next knot up the line tests at 2.7 pounds. In other words, your tippet knot will always break before any of the other knots (assuming all are tied correctly).

Knotless Leaders

Knotless leaders are made by extruding hot nylon and subjecting the pliable material to a complicated series of rolling and stretching operations. The leader is heated and cooled a number of times along the way. The process is computer-controlled, requiring a 50-yard run of machines and not simply an extrusion, as many anglers think. Early knotless leaders were often stretched to the point where the properties of the nylon were changed, almost always to their detriment, and it was impossible to construct a knotless leader with a butt over about .019″ in diameter. Since most experts recommend a leader with at least a .021″ butt for proper performance, early knotless leaders were clearly a compromise. Since about 1990, knotless leaders, particularly the ones coming out of Japan, have improved considerably in butt diameters, taper, and quality control. Most fly fishers now consider them as good as any other type of leader.

The obvious disadvantage of knotless leaders is that, at first glance, they seem to be disposable. Every time you tie on a new fly the leader gets shorter, but it also gets stiffer. Because the diameter of your tippet section can be the most important part of your tackle, it's important to know when the piece to which you're tying your fly is too heavy.

Knotless leaders are manufactured with a level tippet that is somewhere between 2 and 3 feet long, depending on taper and length. Where the tippet ends and the intermediate transition section begins is never a clear division, because there's no knot or even an abrupt change in diameter to tell you. So what do you do after you change flies ten times and feel that your tippet is too thick? Throw away the leader and spend three bucks for another one?

A knotless leader won't gather weeds when you're playing a fish.

For flexibility and convenience as well as economy, you'll want to carry an assortment of tippet spools and gradually turn your knotless leader into a semi-knotless leader. Let's say you are using that 9-foot 4X leader and that you've tied and removed a dozen flies, so you have lost at least a foot of tippet material. That's too short—take my word for it for the time being. Somewhere up along that leader the material widens into .008″ or 3X, the next size up from your 4X. You can find this spot with a micrometer or one of the less expensive feeler gauges made for measuring tippet diameter. However, you don't have to get that fancy. Pull spools of 3X and 4X tippet material out of your fishing vest and hold a piece of 3X alongside your leader, sliding it up along the leader until you get to the point where the diameters look the same. Cut your leader here and tie on a new piece of 4X, anywhere from 2 to 5 feet long. We'll get into the particulars on how long it should be shortly (see page 56).

Eventually, you'll be able to eyeball the diameter of your leader and won't even have to bother with this sliding business.

Braided Leaders

Braided leaders are more correctly called braided-butt leaders, since the tippet end is made from standard solid monofilament. You might also see them called furled leaders. In contrast to knotted and knotless leaders, in which all parts are made from solid monofilament, braided leaders incorporate a butt section made from many tiny filaments, each much smaller than an individual piece of tippet material. Tapers are made by gradually eliminating fibers from the braid as the leader gets closer to the tippet end. At the fine end of the braided section is a permanent loop, to which you attach looped tippet sections. You can either buy packs of looped tippet sections or make them yourself. Store-bought tippets sometimes come with a Bimini Twist in one end, which is a saltwater knot (page 116) used to double the end of a section of line. It's a knot with 100-percent strength, which makes it unique, and if you

monofilament tippet

tapered braid

use the doubled section to tie a knot, you maintain 100 percent of the weaker section's strength. The reason it's used for trout tippets is that it gives the tippet section a nice taper and makes it turn over better.

You can see the obvious convenience of a braided-butt leader. When your tippet gets too short, you just remove it and attach a new one with a loop-to-loop connection: no tying any of those nasty knots! Of course, there is no reason you can't put a permanent loop onto the end of a piece of solid monofilament, other than the fact that loops are a little bulkier in solid mono than in braid.

Braided leaders have other advantages. Because they are more flexible

A braided leader, showing the permanent loop where the solid monofilament tippet is attached (loop to loop).

than solid leaders in the butt section, yet still have the mass and momentum to uncurl, they mimic the casting loop of supple fly line. Because there is no hinged effect between the supple fly line and still leader butt, you preserve the energy of your casting loop. What this gives you is the ability to easily straighten out a 5-foot tippet; with some practice you'll be able to straighten a tippet up to double that length. And the longer your tippet, the more realistic your presentation, because the heavier part of the leader is farther from the fish.

The flexible butt section of a braided leader has another advantage, too. Once the leader hits the water, the conflicting currents pulling at it are less likely to move the fly unnaturally, because its flexibility will bend and absorb the energy of the currents. With a stiffer leader, any current movements at the butt section are more likely to be telegraphed right to the fly—resulting in the unnatural movement of the fly, or drag.

Yet another advantage of braided leaders, a more subjective one, is that some people just like the way they cast, and feel they are much easier to turn over. There is absolutely nothing wrong with choosing a leader this way; try one and see how you like it.

Braided leaders do have some disadvantages. The biggest objection to them is that the hollow braid holds water, and that you throw spray onto the water when you false cast over a fish. This is not a problem in broken or dirty water, but might spook the fish in clear shallow water. Most of the spray can be eliminated by rubbing a small amount of paste fly dressing into the

A braided leader will give you a more natural drift in situations where drag is tricky and a long tippet is needed.

braid, which will keep it from absorbing water. Some braided leaders on the market come pre-treated with a permanent dry silicone treatment.

Because of their flexibility, braided leaders don't work well with big air-resistant flies, with weight on the leader, or with strike indicators. If you think part of your day might involve streamer fishing or casting in pocket water with split shot on the leader and a strike indicator, you might want to start out using a solid leader, unless you feel like changing leaders in the middle of the day. This is not to say you can't fish this stuff with braided leaders, but most anglers reserve braided leaders for fishing with dry flies and nymphs size 12 and smaller.

Poly Leaders

Poly leaders are made by coating a monofilament core with clear, flexible polyethylene. Bigger in diameter than regular monofilament leaders, they have a lower specific gravity and the pure polyethylene ones float. There is a loop in the polyethylene on the end that loops to your fly line; at the other end the nylon core extends from the end of the polyethylene coating and forms a loop to which you can attach a looped tippet section. As with braided leaders, you can make your own or buy tippets with Bimini Twists.

The advantage of poly leaders over braided leaders is that they can't hold water, so they need no dressing and won't throw any water spray. Because they have more mass than other leaders, poly leaders will really punch

monofilament
tippet

tapered
polyethylene
section

a fly with a short tippet, and when you need delicacy they will straighten a tippet up to 8 feet long—which is needed when fish are spooky, because the heavy butt section hits the water pretty hard.

These leaders are best when you need to punch a fly into the wind and when delicacy is secondary. Such situations might occur when you are fishing streamers or weighted nymphs in streams, or when you are fishing stillwater in a wind, where the mass of the leader will help straighten the tippet and the splash of the heavy butt section hitting the water will be masked by waves.

A poly leader, with a larger diameter than regular monofilament. Although the butt section is heavier, a pure polyethylene leader will float. Poly leaders shed water and don't throw any spray.

Sinking Leaders and Mini Lead Heads

Some braided leaders incorporate tungsten slurry into the braid, which produces a fast-sinking leader. Use these the same way you would use an ordinary braided leader, at least as far as attachments are concerned. However, these leaders hit the water hard and should only be used in fast and/or deep water with a short tippet. They are a quick alternative to a sinking or sink-tip fly line when you only need to get a wet fly or streamer a few feet below the surface of the water.

Mini Lead Heads are short pieces of sinking line with loops on both ends. They can be looped to the end of a braided leader or right at the end of the fly line. They offer virtually no delicacy, but neither does a sink-tip line. These are easier to carry in a fishing vest than another fly line and a spare spool for your reel.

Taking a Leader Out of the Package

This may seem like superfluous advice, but I remember that when I started out fly fishing I would invariably tangle a leader when taking it out of a package. Here's how to avoid problems: Take the coiled leader out of the package and insert one hand into the middle of the coils. Find the heavy end, which usually has a loop on it, and work this end out from under the rest of the leader. You'll have to pass it under the coils a half dozen times or so, until you see that it is not wrapped over the rest of the coils. Now slowly pull the heavy end of the leader, letting the coils pay off your hand until the entire leader is free.

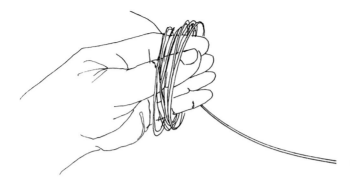

By uncoiling and recoiling a leader this way, you'll avoid tangles.

To put a leader away, simply reverse the process. Start wrapping the tippet end of the leader around the fingers of one hand until you get to about 6 inches from the end. Wrap the heavy end of the leader around the coils four or five times. You can now remove the leader from your fingers and it will stay in a nice neat package.

Chapter 4

LEADER MATERIALS

Prior to the development of nylon in the 1930s, all fly-fishing leaders were made out of silkworm gut, which is exactly what you think it might be. The material was stiff, transparent, and knotted well. But it needed to be soaked prior to use, because it was weak and brittle when dry, and nowhere near as strong as nylon. Gut in 4X diameter (.007″), well soaked, tests at about 1.2 pounds. Modern nylon in this diameter tests at 6 pounds! Like today's knotted leaders, the old gut leaders were made by tying level sections together, but the sections had to be within .001″ of each other in diameter or else the knots wouldn't hold. Not only that, but sections more than 15 inches long were almost impossible to obtain. (How long a strand do you expect you could get from a caterpillar's belly?) Needless to say, old gut leaders were pretty knotty, and when nylon came around most anglers threw their old gut leaders in the trash.

By the way, the "X" sizes we use today refer to the draw-plate gauge sizes used to force the silkworm gut into particular diameters. We still use these terms because they are easier to learn and remember than numbers in thousandths of an inch.

Fly fishermen use diameter rather than pound test because it is the relative flexibility or stiffness of a leader material that matters, not its pound test. If you are fishing a size 8 streamer, a 2X tippet will support the fly and drive it into a stiff wind. On the other hand, a 6X tippet will collapse when tied to the same streamer. Even if you try to tie that thin 6X to the heavy wire on the eye of a streamer hook, the knot will break at a fraction of a pound. In the same light, *if* you could get the 2X tippet through the eye of a size 20 dry fly (and you probably can't), the tippet would slam the tiny fly to the water so hard it would sink. The little fly would be so overwhelmed by the stiffness of the tippet that it would not behave naturally on the water.

Yet you can buy 2X tippet that might test anywhere from 6 to 12 pounds in breaking strength, depending on the formula of the nylon or PVDF. So when choosing tippet material, buy the diameter you need and live with the pound test it offers—or look for another brand that is stronger.

Pound-test ratings are often misleading anyway. When the Orvis product development specialists test different leader materials at independent testing labs, the most important criterion they use for strength in tippet material is pounds-per-square-inch (PSI). Because a 3X tippet might range from .0075″ to .0085″ and still fall within the range that can be called 3X, you can have vast differences in break strength. A .0001″ difference in outside diameter can have a dramatic effect on the mass, and thus the strength, of a piece of round tippet material. Measuring by PSI removes this variable. (This is really only important when you are testing new types of tippet material.)

Tippet material brands differ in suppleness, ability to resist abrasion, ability to remove kinks after being stored on a spool, degree of UV protection, and wet as well as dry knot strength. Unfortunately, the only characteristics that are standardized and measured are dry pound test and diameter. My advice is to buy a reliable brand or one that an experienced fisherman suggests. The bigger companies have the research and development facilities to test and choose the best material.

There are a few brands of tippet material that state their pound tests reliably, but not their diameters. Be careful. Thinking you are fishing 5X when in effect you are fishing something closer to 3X can have a profound negative effect on your fishing success. Unless you plan on carrying a micrometer on the stream, stay clear of brands with unreliable reputations.

Nylon

Most leaders and tippet materials are made from nylon. Typically, a tippet material is made from a copolymer of nylon 6 and nylon 66, with coatings to increase knot strength and protect the material from UV light. Ultraviolet light breaks down nylon, and even with special coatings you should not use any nylon tippet material more than three years old. As of this writing (1999), only Orvis dated its tippet material so the consumer could spot old and potentially weak material that might have sat on the shelf in a fly shop for a couple of years.

In my fishing vest, any nylon tippet material that survives the winter gets thrown out before the first mayfly hatch the following spring.

Nylon has a specific gravity of 1.14—slightly more than water, so it has nearly neutral buoyancy—and

When fishing for large trout with tiny dry flies, most anglers choose a high-strength nylon for its slight edge in breaking strength.

will float if coated with dried algae from the water, oil from your hands, or fly dressing. Sometimes you will want your leader to float—if, for example, you are fishing a dry fly in fast water or an emerger just under the surface. Some anglers feel the shadow of a leader in the surface film spooks trout in calm water, so they rub mud, glycerine, alcohol, or a commercial leader sink onto the material to put it just below the surface and reduce the shadow.

Modern nylons with very strong tensile and knot strength do have some tradeoffs. More tensile strength seems to come at the expense of abrasion resistance and strength after being repeatedly flexed at a severe angle. (This typically happens when fishing a big fly on a light tippet.) This seldom presents a problem when fishing with nymphs and dry flies smaller than size 10, but if you try to use big weighted nymphs or streamers with nylon, especially when casting repeatedly, the material may turn cloudy and brittle. You need to check your tippets constantly when fishing big flies, and replace them often. The other alternative is to switch to a PVDF or fluorocarbon tippet.

PVDF or Fluorocarbon

For a given diameter, a quality nylon material will be the strongest material you can find. However, there will be times when you'll want to use another material, especially if you encounter the abrasion described above. Fluorocarbon or PVDF (polyvinylidenfluoride) is a material used by the packaging industry because it is strong and totally resistant to breakdown by ultraviolet light. Thus you can keep it in your vest forever—and you need to be very responsible and pick up every scrap of it, because it never breaks down. PVDF offers other advantages as well. Its index of refraction is 1.46, extremely close to that of water, which is 1.40. Nylon's index of refraction is 1.72, so nylon is much more visible in water. Serious nymph fishermen consequently swear by PVDF. Also, its specific gravity is 1.26, heavier than nylon's 1.14, so it sinks better, another advantage when subsurface fishing. And finally, PVDF is more abrasion resistant than nylon, so when you are fishing a nymph with split-shot over rocks all day long it holds up better than nylon.

For saltwater species such as striped bass, PVDF material gives extra abrasion resistance, a quick sink rate, and added transparency.

If PVDF offers all these advantages, why not use it all the time? Two reasons: cost and overall strength. PVDF costs about three times as much as nylon, which doesn't sound so bad at 10 bucks a spool, but if you need to carry four or five sizes, the dollars add up. Also, in pure dry break strength, it is theoretically weaker. 4X nylon tests at about 6 pounds and PVDF at 4.75. This is a little misleading, though, because nylon absorbs up to 30 percent water and gets proportionally weaker as it does. PVDF does not absorb water so it loses less in knot strength. In theory, PVDF, when wet and knotted, should be very close to nylon (in the same diameter), but I still think it is just a touch weaker.

Want a recommendation? Use nylon for standard dry-fly fishing, for smaller nymphs in broken water, and for small streamers. Its higher breaking strength will allow you to land and release fish quicker, and you'll save money. If you're fishing nymphs or dries in clear water where trout are fished over heavily, switch to a PVDF tippet for more stealth. And when using big nymphs or streamers with lead on the leader, I would suggest using PVDF for its abrasion resistance. I use it for 100 percent of my saltwater fly fishing, where abrasion resistance is critical.

Don't worry about using a leader with a mixture of nylon and PVDF. They work fine together. Let's say you're fishing a 9-foot 5X knotless nylon leader with a dry fly and you want to fish a small Pheasant Tail nymph over some difficult trout in shallow water. Cut your 5X tippet back to about 6 inches and tie on a 24-inch section of 6X PVDF. For best results, use a triple Surgeon's Knot (page 84) to connect the two different materials.

Chapter 5

MATCHING TIPPET DIAMETER TO FLY SIZE

In the "trout" sizes of tippets, 8X to 0X, each tippet size will handle about three hook sizes properly. Looking at it from a more practical direction, each hook size can be used with about three tippet diameters. The chart below gives you some idea of this range:

TIPPET SIZE	DIAMETER IN INCHES	APPROXIMATE POUND TEST IN NYLON	APPROXIMATE POUND TEST IN PVDF	BALANCES WITH HOOK SIZES
0X	.011	15.5	12	2, 1, 1/0
1X	.010	13.5	10	4, 6, 8
2X	.009	11.5	8	6, 8, 10
3X	.008	8.5	6	10, 12, 14
4X	.007	6	4.75	12, 14, 16
5X	.006	4.75	4	14, 16, 18
6X	.005	3.5	3	16, 18, 20, 22
7X	.004	2.5	2	18, 20, 22, 24
8X	.003	1.75	1	24, 26, 28

Let's look at a size 16 fly. For most "normal" conditions—moderately riffled water, a dry fly that is not too air-resistant, a weighted nymph that is not too heavily weighted—you'd pick the middle tippet, or 5X. If that size 16 fly has oversized hackle or big wings that tend to twist and spin a light tippet, or if it's a weighted nymph or a beadhead that may not let the leader straighten when fished on a lighter tippet, 4X might be better. If the fish are unusually large, you also might want to use the 4X tippet for its greater strength. If you do, make sure you don't use a fly tied on a fine wire hook, as the hook may straighten when fished on the stronger tippet. (Don't we all wish we had the problem of catching fish so big we worry about either breaking the tippet or bending the hook!) On the other end of the scale, if the pool you're fishing offers tricky currents that cause the fly to drag, if the fish are caught and released frequently, or if your fly is a delicate dry pattern that just hovers in the surface film, tie on a 6X tippet. Remember, what you gain in subtlety and stealth you'll lose in strength.

Don't forget you also have tippet *length* in your bag of tricks. You can get greater control in the wind by shortening your tippet, and a more natural float by lengthening it. For instance, when fishing a size 16 lightly hackled dry fly in conflicting currents, with trout in a heavily fished catch-and-release section, you might find that the fish refuse your fly on a 2-foot, 5X tippet. By switching to a 4-foot section of 6X you will have better luck with the same pattern. In fact, this is exactly what I do in such situations, and I have much better luck fiddling with tippets than I do with fly patterns.

More trout refuse flies because of a tippet that is too heavy than for any other reason. This is a bold statement, but I am absolutely convinced it's the truth.

Going to Extremes

Can you use a 2X tippet on a size 12 fly? Sure, so long as you can get the tippet through the hook eye. It won't work well in most trout streams, but in places like Alaska, where guides often say they'd tie the fly line right to the fly if they could get it through the eye, a 2X tippet on a size 12 fly might be fine.

Can you tie a 6X tippet to a size 12 fly? Yes, but I don't advise it. This tippet is slightly bigger in diameter than a hair, and won't offer enough stiffness to turn over a size 12 fly. In fact, the fly will spin the tippet when cast. Then when it hits the water it will flop around as if it has a life of its own—not an altogether bad trick, one that will sometimes make a trout pounce on the fly. But most of the time all it gives you is a bird's nest.

The other problem with tying a fine tippet to a bigger fly comes from the relationship between the diameter of the tippet and the diameter of the wire used to form the eye of the hook. If the tippet is too small in relation to the eye diameter, regular Clinch Knots (page 78) will slip, and you'll have to use a non-slip knot such as a Trilene Knot (page 80). And because the fine tippet is so flexible in relation to the mass of the fly, the tippet is bent repeatedly during casting at an acute angle. This flexing weakens the tippet, the same way bending a piece of soft aluminum too many times does.

Chapter 6

WHY IS TIPPET LENGTH IMPORTANT?

The most valuable trick you'll ever learn in dry-fly and nymph fishing is to use a tippet that is longer than the one provided with your leader. Why don't manufacturers sell their leaders with extra-long tippets? Because they don't "straighten" in the traditional sense, and when people first cast them they think the leader is defective. The reason braided-butt leaders and poly leaders are so effective is that they will straighten these extra-long tippets far better than traditional knotted or knotless leaders will. The reason long tippets are effective, I think, has little to do with visibility, and much to do with flexibility. Trout feed on midges smaller than anything we can tie, so they can see a 7X tippet better than we can. However, if the fly looks natural and if the tippet tied to that fly does nothing to make the fly look unnatural, most times trout ignore the tippet—unless they have been caught and released many times and have learned to associate a piece of nylon tied to a bug with the sensation of being dragged around by the nose for a few minutes. In that case it's time to switch to PVDF.

But most times, a tippet that is too stiff or too short jerks the fly around, causing it to drag or move in ways contrary to the currents that are carrying it.

A fly drifting in the current has some inertia of its own. It takes some force to move the fly contrary to its course with the current that holds it—but not very much. When the heavy fly line gets pushed by conflicting currents, its greater mass will quickly transfer that energy to the leader, and then down the line to the fly. But there is always some slack to take up before the movement reaches the fly, just as the caboose does not move immediately when a locomotive gets started; there is both some inertia to overcome and some slack between the couplings to take up. You can purposely throw some slack into a line and leader to overcome this drag to some degree. But putting more length into the tippet buys even more time before the fly starts to drag, especially when the tippet gets so long that it does not straighten completely.

Putting a big spring between the last car and the caboose will delay the movement of the caboose, and the longer the spring, the longer the delay. And the lighter the spring the longer the delay, too, so long as the spring is not so light that it breaks when trying to move the caboose. This is why we don't use 8X tippet (.003″) all the time. You'll always have fewer problems with drag with 8X tippet than with 4X, but because it breaks at just over a pound, you will have trouble landing all but the smallest trout.

The same concept holds true for nymph fishing, because the object of fishing subsurface flies is to let them sink as quickly as possible while drifting free in the current. In fact, because a nymph is most effective when not pulled by the leader in two dimensions, both upward and across currents, you can argue that a long tippet here is even more effective.

When you impart motion to the fly, such as when stripping a streamer or twitching a nymph through a

A long tippet can help when you're fishing nymphs in fast water with swirling currents.

slow pool or in a lake, a long tippet is not necessary, because you need immediate connection to the fly.

How long should your tippet be? In a non-demanding dry-fly presentation, where you are fishing straight upstream and there are no tricky currents, 2 feet is about right. The same tippet could be used for fishing a nymph in shallow water or an emerger just under the surface. When should you lengthen your tippet? Suppose you move from a riffle to a pool where the surface is contorted into scores of whirlpools and secondary currents. As soon as your fly hits the water, it's dragged across the surface like a water skier. To counter this, lengthen your tippet to 4 feet and throw slack into your presentation by either overpowering the cast and letting it snap back, or by underpowering the cast and letting it fall into loose coils. You will get a much longer drift before the fly begins to drag. If you still get some drag, lengthen the tippet to 5 feet and try again. I have heard of anglers using tippets as long as 15 feet when fishing in back eddies and whirlpools, but for most of us mortals the maximum tippet length should be about 6 feet. Otherwise the cast becomes unruly and the fly will twist the leader into a slinky.

A long tippet is especially helpful when casting to a fish rising in slack water along a far bank, or when you have to fish a nymph or dry fly downstream. You can get a surprisingly drag-free presentation to a trout rising directly downstream by using a 5-foot tippet and a little slack in your presentation.

When is a tippet too long? When your fly starts to twist the tippet, or when you're faced with a headwind that keeps blowing the fly back alongside the fly line, it's time to cut back. If you're unable to place the fly with accuracy, a long tippet won't do you any good either. How does the overall leader length affect the length of the tippet? Not much. Longer leaders keep the fly line farther from the fish, but a 15-foot leader won't straighten a 5-foot tippet much better than a 9-foot leader will. Tippet length is determined more by conditions on the surface of the water than by how far you are casting or by the nervousness of the fish.

Another Option—The Harvey Leader

George Harvey, the Pennsylvania legend who developed the Penn State fly-fishing courses later taken on by the equally innovative Joe Humphreys, has another solution to the problem of drag. Fifty years ago, Harvey did a fascinating study which proved that leader flexibility with its subsequent drag reduction, not the physical diameter of the tippet, is what really affects a trout's acceptance of a fly. He did this by chumming a stretch of Spruce Creek until he had a pod of trout rising. When he threw a beetle with a piece of 5X tippet tied to it into the stream, a trout ate the beetle without hesitation. He then kept chumming but increasing the diameter of the tippet until he was tying tippet more suitable for saltwater fish to the beetles. The fish still ate them, which proved that leader flexibility—combined with casting accuracy—is what counts.

Harvey does not believe in long tippets because they won't straighten in the wind. He builds special knotted leaders with smaller-than-normal butts and mid-sections so the entire leader lands in soft curls that absorb the effects of drag. I happen to disagree with this philosophy, and still prefer the option of adding a long tippet whenever I feel I need it. And I feel I get better accuracy by using a "normal" leader with a long tippet. Now Harvey has eight decades of experience on trout waters, and I only have about four, so I'll let you try both and make up your mind. Differences of opinion are what makes fly fishing so much fun. I know the Harvey leaders will help you catch more trout because they reduce drag.

You can tie your own Harvey leaders with a half-dozen spools of tippet material. The following formula is for a 5X leader just over 11 feet long—perfect for almost any trout-fishing situation. Compare it to the formula for the 9-foot 4X leader earlier in the book and you'll see the great difference in the way this leader is tapered. You can modify it for any tippet size by using the same philosophy mentioned in the section on knotted leaders.

LENGTH	DIAMETER
10"	.017"
18"	.015"
18"	.013"
18"	.011"
18"	.009"
12"	.008"
18"	.007"
24"	.006"

Getting an Edge—Decreasing Your Tippet Diameter While Increasing Its Length

While you can decrease drag by increasing the length of your tippet or by using a Harvey leader, you can accomplish the same thing by decreasing the diameter of your tippet. This increases the flexibility between the fly and the fly line—a lighter spring between the caboose and the last car. One disadvantage of going to a smaller diameter is that you lose breaking strength. Another is that you may have trouble straightening a fly with some air resistance. But with a small fly that is not very air-resistant, with calm winds, you can switch to both a lighter and longer tippet. I'd say that when using a size 14 dry fly, going from a 2-foot 4X tippet to a 4-foot 5X tippet will increase your chances of catching rising fish under difficult conditions by about 30 percent.

Chapter 7

LEADER LENGTH

The philosophy of leader length is to keep your fly line as far as possible from the fly without sacrificing control of where you put your fly. Leaders can be as short as 6 inches and as long as 25 feet. As with most things in life, you'd be well advised to stay away from the extremes; most conventional leaders are between 6 and 15 feet long.

When fishing any kind of sinking line, from sink tips to full sinking lines, most anglers opt for a 6-foot leader for a number of reasons. First, sinking lines do not cast as easily as floating lines and it's harder to turn over a longer leader with a sinking or sink-tip line. Second, because nylon will float if even mildly contaminated with dirt or oil, it defeats the purpose of a sinking line if the leader is trying to pull the fly back to the surface. Shorter leaders keep the fly closer to the sinking line. This is not a concern with PVDF leaders because they sink on their own; regardless, you still seldom need a leader longer than 6 feet, because delicacy is not critical when fishing a fly in deep water. Visibility under water is limited to a few feet, whereas a trout can see a floating fly line as much as 10 feet away in clear water.

Some people use leaders as short as 6 inches, and rather than bothering with a taper, they just loop a tippet right to the loop on the end of a fly line. I'd caution against this unless you are fishing in extremely dirty

Nine-foot leaders are the length most commonly used on medium-sized streams.

water. Whether you are stripping a streamer past a fish or drifting a nymph, the fly line is probably going to brush close to the fish before the fly, which will put a trout on alert.

When fishing with a floating line, a 7½-foot leader is the shortest you'll want, and this length should be reserved for small-stream trout fishing, bass fishing, or fishing big streamers. Bass are not leader or line shy and the only time you might want a longer leader for bass is when you're fishing for smallmouths in clear rivers. In small-stream trout fishing the fly seldom drifts more than 3 feet before you have to pick up and cast again, so you don't need the extra length. Also, a shorter leader turns over better with short casts and your casts in small streams will never be longer than 30 feet. When fishing big streamers with a floating line, a short, stiff leader will turn the fly over more easily and put you in instant control once it hits the water.

In medium-sized streams (over 20 feet in average width) and big rivers, there will be some conditions where you should consider a 7½-foot leader. If it is windy and you are fishing a bulky fly, bigger than a size 10 subsurface fly or a size 14 dry fly, it might be tough to control a 9-foot leader. However, I would advise you to limit a leader this short to broken or discolored water. In clear water in a slow pool, you'll spook more trout than you will be able to interest in your fly.

Nine-foot leaders are the length most commonly used in trout fishing, and they strike a great balance between subtlety and control. For dry flies, nymphs, wets, and streamers smaller than size 8 in most trout streams, especially in riffled water and earlier in the season, a 9-foot leader is all you will need.

When should you go longer and how can you tell? Of course, if you can see trout dive for the nearest submerged log when you cast over them, it does not take a rocket scientist to figure out that you need a longer leader. But seeing trout spook when you cast over them is rare; usually you just don't get any strikes and you figure the fly pattern is wrong.

If you need a rule of thumb, I'd suggest that you go to a 12-foot (or longer) leader any time you have one or more of the following conditions:

- If you are fishing a fly smaller than size 16
- If winds are calm
- If you are fishing water shallower than 3 feet
- If the water has no ripple on it, either from wind or current
- If the river is at its seasonal low-water level
- If the river gets high fishing pressure

The cues to go longer than 12 feet aren't so clear-cut. But I would always use a 15- or 18-foot leader on clear lakes or ponds when using a floating line, so the more pond-like the stream conditions, the more you should consider going to the longest leader you can cast. It's not that you won't get any strikes by not using a 15-foot leader. You might get fewer strikes, though, or that 20-inch brown might turn tail when you cast over him.

Use a long leader—up to 12 feet—when fishing small flies on flat water.

Don't be too concerned about being able to straighten a leader that is 12 feet long or longer. First, a well-designed 12-foot leader will cast as well as a 9-foot leader, provided you are casting more than 25 feet. Also, if you feel the need for a 12-foot leader, you probably don't want the leader to straighten perfectly, because you need some cushion to prevent drag.

Chapter 8

LEADERS AT STREAMSIDE

One of the most important parts of leader skill is the ability to modify a single leader throughout the day or even through a half-dozen trips by adding and subtracting sections. It takes less time to do this than to constantly change leaders, and is far more economical. The most basic modification is to tie on a new tippet of the same size you started with, and we've already covered that in the sections that introduced each type of leader. I have found that it's easiest to start with a 9-foot leader and add sections or cut off pieces as needed.

Be aware that unless you are just adding a new tippet to your leader, you're getting into the trial-and-error world once you start making major modifications to a leader. If you insist on as few knots as possible, which might be necessary in an algae-choked spring creek, or if you want optimum casting performance, you might want to replace your leaders more often.

Going Lighter

You are fishing a size 14 dry fly on a 9-foot knotless leader with a 4X tippet. The leader is fresh from the package and does not have a single knot in it—yet. You see a number of size 20 olive mayflies on the water and the trout start rising. That 4X leader is way too heavy to use with a size 20 dry fly. You need 6X because that .002″ reduction in diameter will change your leader from one that drives the fly crisply to the surface to a leader that settles with a whisper over the trout.

Fold the end of the leader over and eyeball it to find the last place where it seems to be the same diameter as the tippet. Cut the leader there. Using a Barrel Knot (page 86), tie a 6- to 8-inch piece of 5X tippet material to the end of the leader. Now tie your 24-inch 6X tippet to the end of the piece of 5X. Do you see what you've done? You have added a piece of material as a transition. This will allow you to tie another half-dozen 6X tippets onto the leader without having to guess about diameter

Changing a 9-foot 4X leader to a 9-foot 8-inch 6X leader.

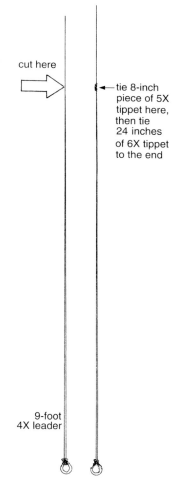

cut here

tie 8-inch piece of 5X tippet here, then tie 24 inches of 6X tippet to the end

9-foot 4X leader

again. Don't worry about fishing a 9-foot 8-inch leader instead of a 9-footer. Nobody will arrest you.

If you wanted to go to a 7X tippet in the above example, you could have tied on an 8-inch section of 5X, an 8-inch section of 6X, and then a 2-foot 7X tippet. Theoretically, you could tie the 7X tippet right to the piece of 5X, but because the tippet-to-leader knot (or the last knot in your leader) is the weakest link in your whole outfit, I like to make sure I am jumping only .001" when tying on my tippet.

With a knotted leader, the whole process is even easier, because you know exactly where to tie on a new section. To make the 9-foot 4X leader to a 6X leader in the example above, you would just turn the tippet into another intermediate section by cutting the tippet 6 inches below the knot that joins it to the rest of the leader, tying on another 6-inch piece of 5X, and then tying your tippet to that. Don't forget that tippet is a relative term and your tippet of 10 minutes ago can become just another humble intermediate section.

Going Longer

It's not practical to turn a 9-foot leader into a 15-footer. With a couple of knots, though, you *can* turn a 9-foot leader into a 12-footer or a 7½-footer into a 9-footer. Let's go back to the original example of the 9-foot 4X leader. As with the other examples, the easiest way to change a leader is to fool with the transition sections. Take out your spools of 2X, 3X, and 4X tippet. Using the

2X material, find the place where the leader first turns to about the same diameter. (If you are using a knotted leader, go back to the place where the 2X transition piece is knotted to the 1X transition piece.) Cut it here, which will be about 30 inches from the end of the leader. Tie in an 18-inch piece of 2X, then an 18-inch piece of 3X, and finally 30 inches of 4X.

Now you have a 12-foot 4X leader, with not quite the same taper as the original leader. The difference between this leader and the original store-bought one is that this one will not turn over quite as crisply, will flutter a little more at the end and might re-

Changing a 9-foot knotless leader into a 12-foot leader.

cut at approximately 1X or .010"

30-inch piece of 4X

18-inch piece of 3X

18-inch piece of 2X

9-foot 4X leader

Use lighter tippets when fishing small flies to selective trout.

quire just a touch more snap at the end of the cast. Many times you won't want the end of your leader to turn over perfectly, especially if drag becomes a problem, so the difference can actually be beneficial.

Modifying Braided Leaders

Many people use braided leaders because of their convenience: When a new tippet is needed, they just take one out of a package and loop it to the leader without tying a knot. Because of the casting dynamics of a braided leader, nearly any tippet can be looped to the end of the braided butt section without any sacrifice in performance. The store-bought tippets with Bimini Twists in them work best because the long Bimini knot gives the tippet itself a gentle taper. You can also buy tippet material and tie your own Bimini tippets but most people don't, because the knot is nasty to tie in small-diameter material; after all, the knot was designed for nylon the diameter of the butt sections of our trout leaders!

You can also just put a Perfection or Surgeon's Loop in the end of a piece of tippet and loop it to the braided leader. It won't perform quite as well as one with a Bimini Knot in it, but the process is quick and easy.

I use a slightly different tippet system on my braided leaders. I

30-inch piece of 6X

8-inch piece of 5X

8-inch piece of 4X

12-inch piece of 3X

cut loop here

Surgeon's Knot

braided leader

braided butt section

Modifying a braided leader.

think loops in the middle of a leader are too bulky, so I tie a couple of pieces of monofilament to the end of the braided butt and use them as transition sections. Here's how to do it if you don't mind tying knots and want optimum performance from your braided leaders: Cut the loop off the thin end of a braided leader and attach a 12-inch piece of 3X tippet to the end of the braid with a double Surgeon's Knot. Trim the tag ends of the knot with a sharp pair of scissors. Tie an 8-inch section of 4X to the end of this. Since I don't use braided leaders with tippets heavier than 5X, I simply tie my tippet to the 4X section. And if I want to go lighter than a 5X tippet, for example to 7X, I tie 8-inch sections of 5X and 6X, then add my 7X tippet.

Going Shorter and Heavier

Most times that you modify a leader you'll be going longer and lighter. But let's say you're in a drift boat, the fish have stopped responding to dries and nymphs, and you want to pound the banks with a big streamer. The only leader in the boat is your 9-foot 5X knotless leader. Cut off the tippet and 2 feet of the leader—you'll have about a 7-foot 2X leader for streamer fishing. If you later decide to go back to dry-fly fishing, you'll have to add an 8-inch section of 3X and one of 4X to get back to the point where you can use a 5X tippet.

Again, it's easier with a knotted leader because you just count back a couple of knots and tie on a 2X tippet. This is why I recommend that you tie your own knotted leaders; you'll know the diameter of each transition section, so you will know exactly where to tie the 2X tippet. If you don't tie your own leaders, carry this book in your fishing vest. Or carry a micrometer.

cut here

9-foot 5X   7½-foot 2X

Changing a 9-foot 5X knotless leader into a 7½-foot leader for streamer fishing.

Chapter 9

SHOULD MY LEADER FLOAT OR SINK?

When You Want Your Leader to Sink

There are conflicting schools of thought on whether a leader should float or sink. When nylon leaders became available after World War II, the floating qualities of the nylon drove fly fishermen nuts. Silkworm gut leaders sink well, and anglers had just gotten used to their leaders sinking. Then someone noticed that a leader floating in the surface film cast a much bigger shadow on the bottom of a stream because of the dimple it causes in the water's surface. Does this spook fish?

I have always been fairly casual about whether my leader floats or sinks, but I remember fishing the Snake River and its productive spring creeks with the legendary Vern Bressler. In these waters thrives an unusually leader-shy and fussy strain of cutthroat trout. After an hour or so of fishing, I'd meet up with Vern and whine that I just couldn't fool any rising fish. "Put any Mud on your leader?" he'd ask. I had to admit I didn't, and after applying some of Vern's top-secret Mud to my leader, I started fooling a lot of fish. At least I thought I did.

Vern concocted his own Mud "from special ingredients mixed only under the light of a full moon." I never did figure out all the ingredients, but I know he used some local Wyoming bentonite clay and a particular brand of denture adhesive. I found out about the adhesive when Vern told me a story about buying pounds of the stuff weekly (Vern sold his concoction to Orvis for years). As he was walking out of the drugstore one morning, he heard the two women behind the counter remarking as to how "that poor old guy must have some real problems with his teeth." As Vern was dying of cancer he turned his secret formula over to a young disabled man who still sells the stuff to Orvis UK. Chalk-stream anglers are always conscious of leader shadow and they swear by Mud over any other leader-sinking potion.

Even though nylon is slightly heavier than water, when left to its own devices it almost always tries to float. Oil from your hands, silicone from fly and line dressings, and just a buildup of algae from rich waters prevent it from sinking. If you don't have access to Vern's secret Mud, anything that removes oil or grease and breaks the surface tension—soap, alcohol, glycerine—will work. Or you can just scrub your leader in regular streamside mud. Common mud is not as good as Mud, but it will do in a pinch.

Modern anglers who are fussy about floating leaders have a far better answer: use PVDF leaders or just a PVDF tippet. This stuff does sink, quite well, because it has a specific gravity of 1.26 as opposed to nylon's 1.14. So if you are fishing a dry fly in flat water and you suspect that the shadow of your tippet is spooking the trout, or at least making them suspicious, the higher cost of PVDF might be worth it. Is a few bucks a spool worth it to you for more rises to your flies over the season? PVDF will also give you an advantage when fishing a nymph close to the bottom.

When You Want Your Leader to Float

There are also times when you want your leader, especially the tippet, to float. The most obvious case is when fishing an emerger fly, a semi-wet fly that should ride just below the surface. Here, a floating tippet will help keep the fly just below the surface where it belongs. Most people grease their tippet to about 6 inches from the fly to accomplish this. Because most of the leader floats, why aren't fish spooked by the leader's shadow? Good question, since this is an especially deadly tactic. It's one reason I usually don't worry about my leader floating at all.

Another place for a floating leader is when you're fishing a dry fly in rough, tumbling water. The countless little swirls in pocket water constantly try to pull the leader, and thus your fly, under water. By greasing your leader with fly or line dressing, you can keep the leader on top of the water and help your fly float longer. Because a leader gliding on top of the water is not tugged as firmly as a leader under the surface, a floating leader in this instance also helps avoid drag. Since there is no worry of spooking the fish with shadows in broken water, I grease my leader all the way to the fly in this situation.

A third place for a greased leader is when you're skating a caddis, a deadly technique when conditions are right. To do this properly the fly must skim lightly across the surface on its hackles, and a leader that pulls the fly under will ruin the presentation.

How to Straighten a Leader

Leaders fresh from the package or from your leader wallet are full of coils. (At least the solid ones are. Braided-butt leaders have almost no memory, a quality that further endears them to their fans.) It's true that you don't always *want* your leader to land perfectly straight, but in such cases the loose coils should be where and when *you* add them to your presentation, and not dictated by the properties of the leader.

The easiest way to straighten a leader is to pull it tightly until it stretches. Start at the butt and work down the leader in sections, lessening the amount of force as you get closer to the fine tippet. If kinks still remain, draw the leader carefully through your thumb and forefinger. The heat generated by the friction will help realign the molecules in the material in the direction you're pulling. Don't do this if your fingers are wet or you have delicate skin, because nylon or PVDF can cut through soft skin.

Don't use a piece of inner tube to straighten a leader, as older books may advise. Inner tubes leave a black rubbery layer on a leader, which not only makes it more visible but keeps it from sinking. If you have trouble straightening leaders by hand, buy a commercial leader-straightening device made out of pure gum rubber or leather, which won't add a black layer. I've also seen recommendations to boil a leader to take the kinks out. Don't. It will weaken the leader considerably. You might as well just dump your whole fly box in the river.

Chapter 10

ATTACHING A FLY TO THE TIPPET

Clinch Knot

This is the traditional knot for tying monofilament to any loop. It is most often used to tie the tippet to the eye of the fly, but it is sometimes used with dropper flies to either connect the dropper to the bend of the hook or to the standing part of the leader itself, above a knot. It is strong and reliable but must be tied carefully. When using PVDF material or when tying a tippet to a fly where the diameter of the tippet is much smaller than the wire diameter of the eye, I recommend either the Orvis Knot (page 81) or the Twice-Through-the-Eye Clinch or Trilene Knot (page 80). Both of these knots are superior to the Improved Clinch Knot, a version of the Clinch Knot that is not worth learning.

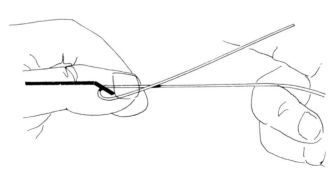

1. Pass the tippet through the eye of the hook. It doesn't matter whether you come from above or below. Place the thumb and forefinger of your left hand in front of the eye to keep a loop open. Cradle the standing part of the line in the last two fingers of your right hand.

2. Wind the tag end around the standing part of the line by using the thumb and forefinger of your right hand to do most of the work. Use the third finger of your left hand to help pass the tag end around the standing part. All of this sounds complicated and you may develop your own method, but by using your fingers precisely as shown, this knot becomes very easy. Use five complete turns for monofilament in diameters from .007″ to .017″. Use three turns for shock tippets, because you will never get the coils to tighten in the heavy stuff and three turns seem to hold well. In material smaller than .007″ in diameter I use seven turns, because the smaller stuff seems to slip more easily.

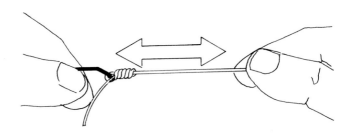

3. Pass the tag end through the loop you have held open in front of the eye. Lubricate the knot with saliva and draw it tight with a quick pull on the fly and the standing part of the tippet. Let go of the tag end when tightening this knot. Trim the tag end very close to the knot.

Twice-Through-the-Eye Clinch Knot or Trilene Knot

I use this knot mainly for bigger flies. Although this is my favorite for tying saltwater flies to a regular tippet (not a shock tippet), it's also great when fishing big nymphs, streamers, or bass flies. The knot is trickier to tie and tighter than the Clinch Knot.

1. Start this knot the same way as you would start a Clinch Knot, but after you have brought the tippet through the hook eye, keep coming around and pass the tippet through the hook eye a second time, in the same direction as the first pass. This

will form a double loop in front of the eye as you start to make your turns around the standing part of the line. Keep this loop open with the thumb and forefinger of your left hand.

Tying a Trilene Knot (modified Clinch Knot—twice through the eye).

2. Wind the tag end around the standing part *five times only*. Bring the tag end back through the double loop in front of the eye.
3. Moisten and tighten carefully. Instead of letting go of the tag end as you would when tightening a Clinch Knot, it helps to hold the tag end tightly against the fly.

Orvis Knot

This is a small, strong knot that is hard to tie incorrectly once learned. It is superb for all freshwater applications, and for tying saltwater flies to the tippet when you are not using a shock tippet.

81

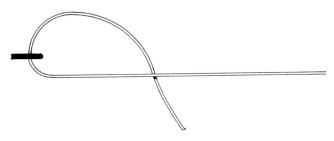

1. Give yourself plenty of tippet for this one. Pass the tippet through the eye of the fly from the bottom and form a loop by bringing the tag end over the standing part of the tippet on the *far* side.

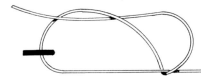

2. Form a second loop, farther away from the fly, by bringing the tag end all the way around the standing part, then passing the tag end through the first loop from the *far* side.

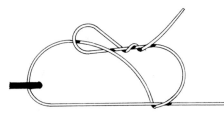

3. Fold the tag end over and take two turns around the loop just formed (the second loop). Make sure these turns start at the *far* side of this second loop.

4. Lubricate the knot. Tighten the second loop against the standing part by pulling on the fly and the tag end. Then let go of the tag end and pull on the fly and the standing part until the knot snugs neatly against the eye. Trim the tag end close to the fly.

Chapter 11

TYING LEADER MATERIAL TOGETHER

Surgeon's Knot

This is one of the easiest knots to tie. It is also one of the strongest, and unlike the Barrel Knot (p. 86), it can be used to join sections that are as much as .004″ different in diameter. Its only disadvantage is its bulk; in sections heavier than .012″ the Barrel Knot is much neater and smaller.

1. Overlap the tag ends of the two strands you are joining by 4 to 6 inches. The section not attached to the rest of your leader and line (in most cases a new tippet) should start in your left hand.

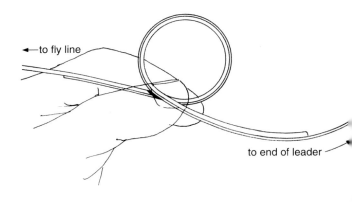

←—to fly line

to end of leader —

2. Form a loop in the overlapped strand and pinch the junction of the loop with the thumb and forefinger of your right hand.

3. Using your left hand, wrap the standing part of the tippet (or smaller piece) and the tag end of the bigger piece through the loop three times. Treat them as a single piece; they'll stay together easier if you wet them with saliva. Many sources recommend using only two turns, but lab tests have shown us that the Triple Surgeon's Knot is marginally stronger and no harder to make with a third turn.

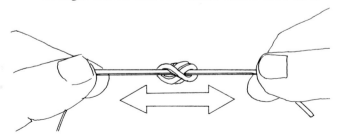

4. Tighten this knot by holding both short and long ends on each side and pulling quickly and tightly. Make sure all strands are snug, then trim the tag ends as close to the knot as possible.

Barrel or Blood Knot

This knot is used to make knotted leaders. The knot is neat and clean, and nearly as strong as the Surgeon's Knot when tied carefully. The sections joined should differ by no more than .002″ in diameter. (In other words, you can join 2X to 4X but not 1X to 4X.)

1. Cross the two strands of monofilament, forming an **X**. This knot is easier to tie if there are 5 to 6 inches of tag end on each side of the **X**.

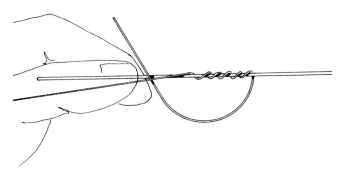

2. Cradling the standing end of each strand in the last two fingers of each hand, start by winding the tag end of one strand around the standing part of the other strand, working away from the **X**. Use your thumb and forefinger to make these turns. Keep the loop formed at the **X** open by pinching it with the thumb and forefinger of the hand you are not using to wind. In this knot, unlike the Surgeon's Knot, it doesn't matter which hand holds the heavier strand, and the smaller end does not have to pass through the knot; if you already have a fly tied onto your tippet, this knot is easier.

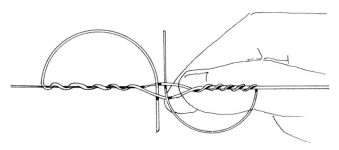

3. Use three turns on each side with monofilament bigger than .017″ in diameter. With material from .015″ to .010″ in diameter, use five turns; and for material .009″ in diameter and smaller, use a full seven turns. Pass the end you have just been winding through the loop at the **X**. Now pinch the loop with the thumb and forefinger you have just

been using to wind. Try to keep the loop open, because the tag end from the other side will have to pass back through this loop. Repeat the process on the other side, making sure you wind *the same number of turns* on both sides. Pass the second tag end back through the same loop as the first tag end, *from the opposite side of the loop.*

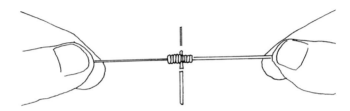

4. Make sure that the tag ends stick out from the loop enough so that they don't slip out when you tighten the knot. Don't pull on these tag ends when tightening the knot. Moisten the knot and pull on both standing parts quickly. The barrels on both sides of the knot should form neat coils; if not, cut the strands and start over.
5. Trim the tag ends close to the knot.

Orvis Tippet Knot

A variation of the Orvis tippet-to-fly knot, developed by Orvis CEO Perk Perkins, can be used to join two pieces of tippet; as in the Surgeon's Knot, the tippets can be up to .004″ different in diameter. This is a very strong knot, with close to 100 percent of the break strength of the weaker strand, but like the Surgeon's Knot, it is bulkier than the Barrel Knot and is best used with larger diameters. If you can tie a Surgeon's Knot, this one is only slightly more difficult.

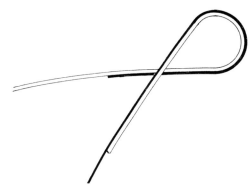

1. Line up both strands with about 8 inches of overlap. Form a loop by bringing the tippet end (and the short end of the heavier piece along with it) around in front of the crossover.

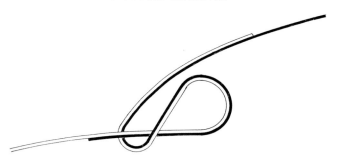

2. Bring these pieces around the back and up, forming an open loop. At this point it helps to pinch the second, open loop.

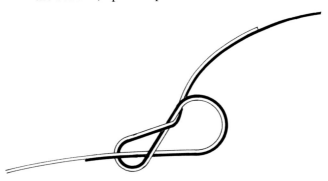

3. Coming around the front of the first loop, close the second loop by bringing the tippet (and the short end of the heavier piece) through the first loop.

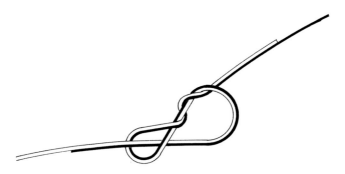

4. Keep going around in the same direction for a second turn.

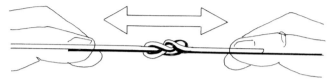

5. Moisten the knot and tighten it by holding both pairs of long and short ends and pulling them against each other at the same time. Trim the tag ends as closely as possible.

Chapter 12

TYING LOOPS IN MONOFILAMENT

Perfection Loop

This knot makes a neat, small loop, ideal for putting a loop in the end of a leader. The Perfection Loop lies perfectly in line with the standing part of the line and as far as we know, it is the only loop knot that can make this claim. It is difficult to tie at first, so follow the instructions carefully. The secret is to make sure that the tag end is always pointing at a right angle to the standing part of the leader.

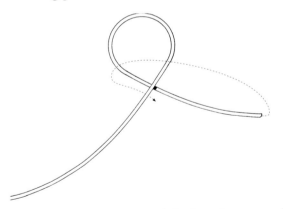

1. Form a single loop by bringing the tag end behind the standing part of the leader. The tag end should be pointing toward the right, at a right angle to the standing part of the line.

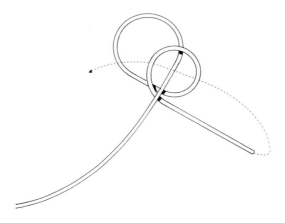

2. Form a second, smaller loop in front of the first one by rolling the tag end around the front of the first loop, then behind it. Push the second loop flat against the first with your thumb, and make sure the tag end ends up on the right side again, pointing at a right angle away from the standing part.

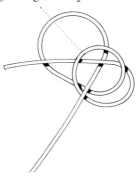

3. Take the tag end and fold it to the opposite side, passing it between the two loops. It should end up on the left, pointing at a right angle to the standing part of the line. Push it to the bottom of the point where the two loops overlap. Pinch it in place here with your thumb.

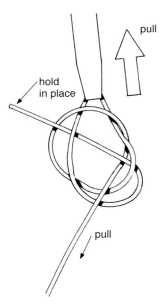

4. Reach behind the first loop and pull the second smaller loop through it. Make sure the tag end stays put, on the left at a right angle to the standing part. Tighten the knot by pulling the second loop straight in line with the standing part of

the leader. Do not hold the tag end or put pressure on it.

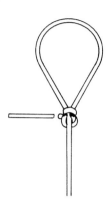

5. Tighten the knot fully and inspect it. The tag end should still be pointing at a right angle to the standing part of the leader and the loop itself should be in line with the standing part. If not, cut the knot and try again. Trim the tag end when you are satisfied the knot is tied properly.

Surgeon's Loop

The Surgeon's Loop is simply a double overhand knot, one that's very strong but not as neat as a Perfection Loop. It is most often used to form a loop in a trout-sized tippet (for instance, when making a tippet section for a braided-butt leader) or for making a loop in a tippet that has been doubled with a Bimini Twist. Its bulk does not matter in these smaller sizes, and because tippet material is not as stiff as butt material, you can't tell that the loop is not in line with the standing part.

1. Make a loop and overlap the tag end with the standing part of the leader for about 5 inches. Pinch the material close to the top of the loop and near the bottom of the overlap.

2. Tie a loose overhand knot in the doubled section and pass the single loop through the double loop you have just formed. Don't tighten.

3. Make another turn of the single loop through the doubled loop. In other words, make a double overhand knot in the doubled section.

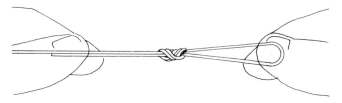

4. Moisten the knot. Tighten it by pulling the loop away from both the tag end and the standing part of the line. Make sure you pull equally on the standing part and the tag end of this knot, unlike the Perfection Loop. Trim the tag end closely.

Chapter 13

TIPS FOR TIGHTENING KNOTS

- To eliminate friction, always wet your knot with water or, better yet, saliva, before tightening the knot. Friction developed between pieces of tippet material creates heat, which can weaken a knot and cause pigtails in your tippet.
- Unless otherwise directed in specific knot-tying instructions, tighten knots quickly but without jerking. A smooth, quick pull, like pulling a cap off a pen, is about right. If you tighten slowly, you'll generate more friction in the knot.
- When tying knots, make sure there is no tension on either the tag end or standing end. Pigtails in front of a fly are usually formed because the line is hanging in the current and pulling on the leader as you tie your knot. This tension pulls the leader across the eye of the fly, thus creating a pigtail. Get slack in the leader by pulling in some line and tucking it under your arm before you start tying.
- Don't be cheap with leader material. It is much harder to tie a knot when you are near the end of a piece of tippet than when you have generous excess.
- If you are over 40, do not ever attempt to tie a critical knot without lots of light and close-up glasses. You lose resolution when wearing sunglasses, so take them off before you put on your

close-up glasses. If you get stuck without glasses at dusk, hold your work against the skylight.

- Practice new knots at home with lots of light and heavy material—not at streamside. Use old fly line instead of tippet material for your first attempts.

- Always test your knots with what you think is appropriate force. For a trout fly tied to a 7X tippet, it might be a gentle pull. For a tarpon leader, it should be about as hard as you can yank. Better to find a weak knot before you make your first cast.

Chapter 14

TIPS FOR CARE OF LEADERS AND TIPPET

- Oxidizing agents such as ultraviolet light and ozone break down nylon very quickly. Never store nylon in direct sunlight or near fluorescent lights or electric motors. This is not a problem with PVDF.
- Solvents in insect repellents and fly flotants can weaken nylon in a heartbeat. If you get any solvents on your hand, rub your hand in streamside mud before touching your leader. I apply insect repellent by using the backs of my hands, not my palms, so that I know I won't ever touch my leader with it. This is not supposed to be a problem with PVDF, but I still don't trust insect repellents.
- An overhand casting knot or "wind knot" in your tippet can weaken it by as much as 50 percent. Don't try to pick it out—the damage is done. Replace the tippet unless you don't care about losing flies and fish. Overhand knots in the heavier section of the leader are not as critical to remove, because they are not weak links. (If you are fishing a 5X tippet that breaks at 4.75 pounds and the 1X section farther up the leader has a wind knot in it, the 1X will still break at one-half of 13.5 pounds, or 6.75 pounds).
- Inspect tippets for areas that looked crazed or opaque, especially right in front of the fly. These

are places where the tippet has been weakened by repeated flexing or abrasion, or by coming in contact with insect repellent. They will break at a fraction of the strength of fresh tippet and should be replaced immediately—not after the next cast!

wind knot here must be removed

wind knot here doesn't matter

A Wind Knot in the heavier section of your leader is not as much of a problem as one in your tippet. Replace the tippet before it breaks.

Chapter 15

LEADERS FOR BASS, PIKE, SALMON, AND STEELHEAD FISHING

Leaders for Bass Fishing

Largemouth bass do not seem to be bothered by tippets of any diameter. Also, when you're fishing a fly for largemouths, *you* are moving the fly, not the current, so flexibility is of no importance. This is a lucky coincidence, because flies for largemouths are huge and air-resistant, and you often have to pull a largemouth from thick tangles of aquatic vegetation. Even a fly line landing right over a largemouth does not seem to bother it, so a leader that is 6 feet long is fine.

I usually use an old knotless trout leader cut back to about 6 feet for largemouths. By the time you cut a 12-footer back to this length it's about .015″ and 25-pound test—stiff and strong enough for any largemouth. If you don't fish for trout or don't have any old knotless leaders, you can make a nice bass leader from a level piece of .015″ or .017″ tippet. PVDF works a little better because of its abrasion-resistant properties. Avoid knotted leaders for largemouths because they pick up weeds. You should use finer leaders for smallmouth bass, particularly in streams. When fishing dry flies, nymphs, and streamers smaller than size 6, a 9-foot leader in 2X to 0X will work fine. If you go to bigger poppers for smallmouths, make your leader shorter and stiffer, as you would for largemouths.

Leaders for Salmon Fishing

Atlantic and Pacific salmon, like bass, don't seem to be leader-shy. Also, you *want* your fly to drag when fishing for these species, so flexibility is not an issue. Particularly with Atlantic salmon, you want the fly to begin dragging and swinging as soon as it hits the water, so a leader with the standard 20-inch tippet is desirable. A 7½- to 9-foot leader with a 0X tippet will get you through most salmon-fishing circumstances, and will test at around 15 pounds, which will let you land the majority of fish with ease. You might want to cut this leader back a couple of feet when using a big double-hook fly. Conversely, you might want to add a piece of 1X or 2X tippet when using small nymphs or low-water flies for Atlantics, or when fishing egg patterns and nymphs for Great Lakes or Pacifics.

Leaders for Steelhead Fishing

Although steelhead and Pacific salmon can be found in the same pools and take the same flies, leaders used for steelhead should have lighter tippets, particularly when you're fishing nymphs or dead-drifting small wet flies. Steelhead seem to be quite leader-shy, and when the water is cold they may not take a fly unless it is drifting completely drag-free, so you need to present the fly more as you would for trout than for salmon. When fishing for winter steelhead in clear water, you may have to go as light as 4X or 5X even though the fish might be over 15 pounds! In this case, a 9-foot 4X or 5X standard trout leader would be appropriate.

Winter steelhead require relatively light leaders with PVDF tippets.

When fishing steelhead flies with weight on the leader, anglers often place a knot or a three-way swivel between the tippet and the rest of the leader and then put the weight on a separate dropper. This way if the weight snags on the bottom, it can be broken off without losing the fly and tippet. Most anglers prefer PVDF tippets for steelhead, both for the abrasion-resistance they offer when fishing close to the bottom and for the added stealth needed for steelhead.

Leaders for Pike Fishing

Although a pike's teeth look sharp, they are nowhere near as serious as those of a bluefish or barracuda. Still, a big pike can cut through a tippet lighter than

.015″, so most people use a heavy bass leader, adding a 12-inch piece of heavier material to turn it into a shock or bite leader. Because pike, like bass, are not leader-shy, you could probably make it simple and just tie a piece of .017″ to .019″ monofilament to the end of your fly line.

You may want to make things more sporting, or perhaps try to set the 12-pound-test record for northerns or muskies. In this case, take your standard 12-pound bass leader and tie a foot-long piece of .019″ PVDF to the end of the leader with an Improved Barrel Knot. (The Improved Barrel Knot is simply a standard Barrel Knot with the smaller-diameter section folded over and doubled before tying the knot.) This heavier piece at the end lets you fish a rig with a breaking strength of 12 pounds, but gives you greater protection where the fish inhales the fly.

I do recommend PVDF for the shock tippet, even though many articles and books might tell you to use "hard monofilament." PVDF is much denser, harder, and more abrasion resistant than any formula of nylon. Why sacrifice a nice fish to save a few pennies on tippet material?

Chapter 16

SALTWATER LEADERS

A saltwater leader can be as simple as a single strand of 20-pound-test monofilament tied to the fly line with a Nail Knot. The best striped bass fisherman I know uses this method about 90 percent of the time, and he has probably caught more striped bass on a fly, and more big bass, than anyone I know. But he fishes in the surf, where the splash of a heavy leader will never spook fish. In most cases you'll want some taper in your leader to slow down the delivery of your fly and make it land without too much commotion.

Saltwater leaders should range from about 6 feet long for stripers in the surf or redfish in dirty water to 15 feet for spooky fish in shallow water. Bonefish guides in Florida sometimes use leaders this long, and I use them regularly for stripers in shallow water. Needless to say, you should shorten your leader for easy casting as the wind picks up—the fish won't be as spooky in riffly water anyway.

If you need to lengthen a saltwater leader, you should lengthen the butt and not the tippet. For instance, let's say you are fishing for redfish on the flats with a 7½-foot leader and you seem to be spooking the fish no matter how carefully you cast. Remove your leader from the line by unslipping the loops, and cut the loop off your leader. Tie 4 or 5 feet

of 25- or 30-pound monofilament (eyeball the butt of your leader and match it, or go slightly heavier) to your leader with a Surgeon's Knot. Tie a Perfection Loop onto the end of the new piece and re-attach it to the line.

Knotless Leaders

For most saltwater species that don't have sharp teeth (stripers, redfish, bonefish, permit, bonito, and false albacore), you can use a factory-made knotless tapered leader made from nylon or PVDF. For bonefish, permit, and redfish, especially where there are either weeds or coral in the water, a knotless tapered leader is recommended by most guides. Knots catch on weeds and ruin your presentation; they catch on coral and, well, *ping!* When the leader gets too short or too heavy, you can replace it or risk the annoyance of a knot and tie on a new tippet, just as you would for a trout leader.

Three-Knot Leaders

For a simple knotted leader, perfect for striped bass or redfish (or bonefish over sand bottoms), tie a Perfection Loop in a 3-foot piece of .017″ PVDF (about 25 pounds). Tie this to a 3-foot piece of .013″ PVDF (about 15 pounds) and then add a 3-foot piece of .011″ (12 pounds) for the tippet. The sections should be joined with Surgeon's Knots.

Class Tippets

By International Game Fishing Association (IGFA) rules, your tippet must be at least 15 inches long between knots if you want your catch to be eligible for the record books. It's tough to determine if a knotless leader has a level piece of class tippet, so most people going for records attach a separate class tippet that has a Bimini Twist in it. Why the Bimini? The weakest link in your leader will probably be the knot where the tippet attaches to the rest of the leader, so you want to tie that knot with a doubled section of the weaker strand. This way the overall breaking strength of your entire rig is 100 percent of the breaking strength of the class tippet.

3 feet of .011" PVDF

Surgeon's Knots

3 feet of .013" PVDF

3 feet of .017" PVDF

The three sections of this 9-foot knotted leader are joined with Surgeon's Knots.

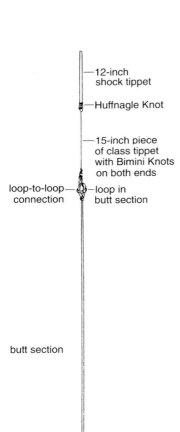

12-inch
shock tippet

Huffnagle Knot

15-inch piece
of class tippet
with Bimini Knots
on both ends

loop-to-loop
connection

loop in
butt section

butt section

The easiest way to do this is to tie a Bimini Loop onto one end of the tippet and then knot this doubled piece to the butt section of your leader. In the three-knot leader above, for example, you'd tie the doubled 12-pound-class tippet to the .013" section with a Surgeon's Knot. A better way to do it is to tie a Perfection Loop onto the end of the .013" section. Tie up a bunch of tippets with Bimini Loops on them ahead of time. Put a Bimini in one end of each tippet, and then tie a Surgeon's Loop in the doubled section—you will end up with a loop with four strands. These

This class tippet with Bimini Twists at both ends is attached to the shock tippet with a Huffnagle Knot (see Chapter 17) and to the butt section of the leader with a Surgeon's Loop.

110

can be rolled around your hand like a leader for storage and kept in a leader wallet or small zip-lock bag until needed. In the heat of fishing, you can slip on a new tippet without tying any knots except for the knot that attaches your fly to the tippet.

Shock Tippets

For fish with moderately sharp teeth or abrasive mouths (such as mackerel, dorado, tarpon, big snook, tuna, and sailfish), you'll need to attach a monofilament shock tippet (PVDF is better than nylon) to the class tippet. These species don't chop through tippet

Because of their abrasive mouths and sharp gill plates, even small tarpon require a shock tippet on the leader.

the way sharks or bluefish do; instead their abrasive mouths wear through the tippet over the course of a long battle, and you need a big-diameter material to cushion against breakoffs.

A single strand of tippet won't join securely to a piece of 50- to 100-pound test material, so you will need to prepare class tippets with Bimini Twist Loops (page 116) on both ends. One end gets a Surgeon's Loop so it can be looped to the butt section of the leader while the other end is permanently tied to the shock tippet with a Huffnagle Knot (page 120). In practice, few people try to tie up shock tippet/class tippet combinations while tarpon are cruising past the boat. These pieces are tied up before a trip, in the calm comfort of your home. Many anglers tie these doubled Bimini sections to a shock tippet, attach a fly to the shock tippet, and store them in a stretcher box that keeps the leader straight. When a fish breaks off or a fly gets ruined, it's a quick step to loop a new class tippet/shock tippet/fly combination to the butt section with a loop-to-loop connection.

Wire Tippets

Sharks, barracuda, wahoo, and bluefish need a wire tippet. I have seen sharks and bluefish bite through 80-pound-test shock tippet before I have even felt the strike. Some newer forms of nylon-coated wire are very flexible and can be used like regular monofilament.

A wire shock tippet will keep sharks from biting through your leader.

Braided wire is joined to the class tippet with an Albright Knot and to the fly with a Homer Rhode Loop (page 123).

Solid wire needs to have a loop put on each end: One loop goes through the eye of the fly and the other loop attaches to the class tippet with a Clinch Knot or Orvis Knot. This loop is made with a Haywire Twist (page 127). Wire tippets should be from 4 to 8 inches long, depending on the size of the fish.

Chapter 17

SALTWATER KNOTS

Albright Knot

This is a traditional saltwater knot that can be used to join materials that are quite different in diameter or to join two different kinds of materials. It is sometimes recommended for joining backing to fly line (I like a Nail Knot better) or to join a shock tippet to a class tippet (a Huffnagle is much better, though). The only place I use an Albright is to join a piece of braided wire to the tippet. This is one of those knots that must be tied and tightened precisely or it will slip.

1. Bend a loop in the tag end of the heavier leader material or wire, allowing at least 4 inches of overlap. Pass the lighter material through this loop and pinch it against the heavier material about 2 inches from the end. You should leave yourself at least 3 inches of material to work with beyond this point.

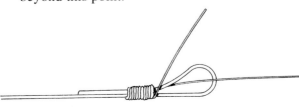

2. With smooth turns, wind the smaller material over the doubled section of bigger material, working toward the loop. Make at least 12 turns.

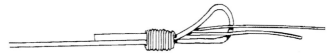

3. Pass the smaller material through the loop on the same side of the loop that it entered.

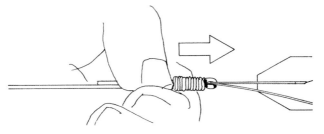

4. Slowly pull on the standing parts of the lighter material and heavier material (this is one knot that should never be tightened quickly!) and work the coils toward the end of the loop, being careful that they don't slip off the end. When the coils are near the end, pull gently on the tag end of the smaller material to snug the coils, then pull gently on the standing part of the lighter material. Keep alternating between pulling on these ends until the knot is tightened neatly against the loop. Now use a pair of pliers or forceps to hold the tag end as you take one last tight turn. Pull

hard on the standing part of the light and heavy ends to make sure the knot will not slip. You can't be too careful with this one. Trim the tag ends of the heavy and light materials.

Bimini Twist

The Bimini Twist is a unique knot because it is not used to join anything. It is used to form a double strand in a piece of monofilament, and it is a 100-percent knot. Why do you want this?

When you join two pieces of material together, you never get a knot that is completely 100 percent—in other words, if you join a piece of 12-pound monofilament to 16-pound monofilament, the resulting strand will break at the weakest link, the knot, and the strength of that link will be about 11.4 pounds, or 95 percent of the weaker piece. But if you double the 12-pound section with a Bimini Twist, the weakest link is somewhere in the middle of the 12-pound section; the breaking strength of the strand will be 12 pounds if there are no nicks or wind knots in the leader.

This becomes important when fishing for the record books, where you want your class tippet (the one you send in to the IGFA when you apply for the record) to break at no more than 12 pounds, but you want every bit of that 12 pounds.

1. IGFA class tippets must have a minimum single-strand section of 15 inches. I find that I need about 6 feet of material to start if I am putting a Bimini on one end only; if I am putting a Bimini on both ends of the tippet, I might need 10 or 12 feet. Double the strand and put one hand through the loop. The other hand pinches the tippet in the middle of the section. Put at least 25 twists in the tippet by rotating your hand, letting the loop slip over the back of your fingers as you do.

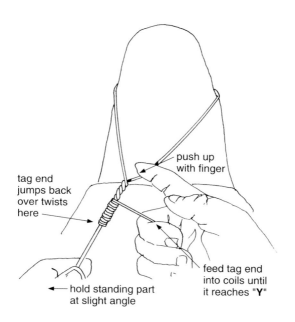

push up with finger

tag end jumps back over twists here

feed tag end into coils until it reaches "**Y**"

← hold standing part at slight angle

2. Slip the loop over your knee. Hold the standing part of the tippet with one hand. Now grab the tag end with the last three fingers of your other hand and place the forefinger of this same hand at the Y formed where the loop meets the twists. Now comes the trickiest part: By holding the standing end just a bit off the vertical, and the tag end at about 90 degrees away from the twists, push your finger gently against the fork of the Y while slowly releasing the tag end. You want the tag end to roll over the twists, toward your forefinger, in smooth even coils. Getting the twist started is the hardest part—once it starts rolling, it helps to move the hand holding the tag end upward to keep the coils neat. Most experts agree that a Bimini is tied correctly only when the coils are jammed tightly against each other so tightly that it looks like a solid piece. Don't let the coils jump over each other, either; there must be a single tight layer of them all the way to the forefinger. Keep rolling these coils until you reach the fork of the Y.

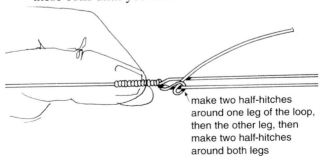

make two half-hitches around one leg of the loop, then the other leg, then make two half-hitches around both legs

3. Pinch the twisted section to keep it from unraveling. Tie a single half-hitch or overhand knot around one leg of the loop and tighten the knot up against the twists. Repeat with the other leg of the loop. Now you can remove the loop from your knee. At this point, if your tag end is longer than 4 inches, it's easier to finish the knot if you cut the tag end back. Tie a half-hitch around both legs of the loop and tighten. Tie another one around both legs and tighten.

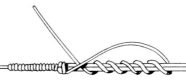

4. Tie one final half-hitch around both legs, but in this case wind five times around both legs of the loop before tightening. You should be working back toward the coils. Tighten by moistening the knot and pulling the tag end up toward the coils. You will have to tighten a bit, work the turns back away from the coils with your fingernail, tighten a bit more, and keep going until the final turns are tight. If you don't back off the turns as you tighten, they won't tighten smoothly. Once the turns are neat and secure, give the tag end a good snugging with a pair of pliers, pulling it toward the closed end of the loop.

finished Bimini Knot

Huffnagle Knot

This is the neatest and most secure way of tying a heavy monofilament shock tippet to a section of class tippet that has been doubled with a Bimini Twist. It is far superior to an Albright Knot for this purpose.

shock tippet

1. Make a double overhand knot in the shock tippet, about 2 inches from the end of the tippet.

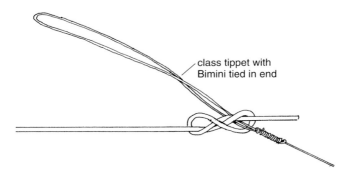

class tippet with Bimini tied in end

2. Tighten this knot until it forms a figure-8, but leave both loops open because you will need to pass the class tippet through both of them.

120

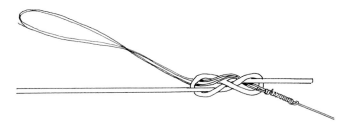

3. Pass the loop at the end of a class tippet (to which you've already tied a Bimini Twist) through the loop of the figure-8 in the shock tippet. The class tippet should first be passed through the loop closest to the end of the tag end of the shock tippet and it should leave the loop through the same side where the tag end exited.

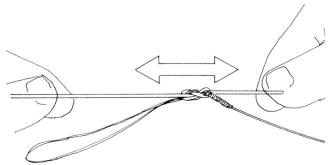

4. Pass the class tippet through the second loop in the figure-8, again entering the loop on the same side that the standing part of the shock tippet exits.

121

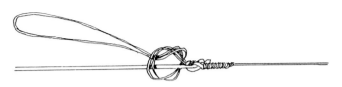

5. Slide the figure-8 up against the Bimini Twist Knot and tighten it by pulling on both ends of the shock tippet. Trim the tag end of the shock tippet.

6. You will notice that the rest of this knot is the same as finishing a Bimini Twist, so if you have mastered that knot, this one will be a snap. Make an overhand knot with the class tippet around the shock tippet. Tighten. Make another overhand knot and tighten.

completed Huffnagle Knot

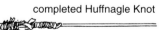

7. Make a third overhand knot, but this time take five turns around the shock tippet, working back toward the figure-8. Tighten this, like the Bimini Twist, by pulling on the tag end, stroking the coils back toward the standing part of the shock tippet to keep the coils from wrapping over

themselves, and repeating until the coils are snug against the rest of the knot. Tighten completely by pulling the tag end toward the class tippet, by pulling on the tag end of the class tippet and the standing part of the shock tippet.

Saltwater Loop Knots

Because saltwater leaders are usually made from heavy material, tying the fly to the tippet with a loop lets the fly swing freely and gives it more action. Two knots are needed: one for heavy shock tippet (40- to 100-pound monofilament, and plastic-coated wire) and one for standard class tippets (from 4 to 20 pounds). The Homer Rhode Loop is easy to tie but weak, so it is used on the heavier stuff. The knot tests at only 50 percent, but with an 80-pound shock tippet it will still be stronger than the class tippet by a comfortable margin. The Non-Slip Mono Loop is trickier to tie, but it tests at nearly 100 percent, even with 1-pound-test material.

Homer Rhode Loop

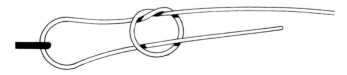

1. Make an overhand knot in the tippet, about 6 inches from its end. Insert the tag end of the leader through the hook eye.

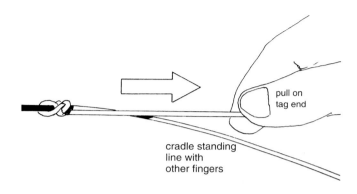

pull on
tag end

cradle standing
line with
other fingers

2. Pass the tag end of the leader back through the overhand knot, making sure that it enters the loop on the same side it exited after you tied the overhand knot.

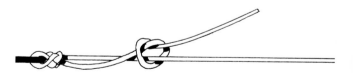

3. Tighten the overhand knot loosely against the eye of the hook by holding the fly in one hand and both pieces of the leader material in the other hand. Cradle the standing part of the leader with the last two fingers of this hand and pull on the tag end with your thumb and forefinger.

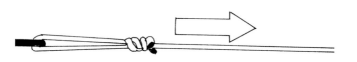

4. Now make another overhand knot with the tag end around the standing part of the leader. Position this knot at the point where you want your loop to end; about ¾ inch to 1 inch is the standard size. This knot should be seated tightly against the standing part of the leader.
5. Pull on the fly and the standing part of the leader. The first knot will jam up against the second knot. Trim the tag end.

Non-Slip Mono Loop

1. Start this knot just as you would a Homer Rhode Loop, by making an overhand knot in the leader before doing anything with the fly. In this case, you should allow about 10 inches of tag end. Don't tighten the loop. Pass the tag end of the leader through the hook eye.

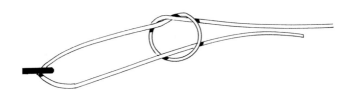

2. Bring the tag end back through the overhand knot, making sure that it enters the loop formed by the overhand knot on the same side as it exited when you tied the overhand. The distance between the fly and the overhand knot determines the size of your loop, so work the knot up or down the standing part of the leader until you get the size loop you want.

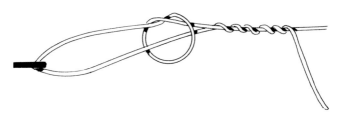

3. Wrap the tag end around the standing part of the leader, just as you would in tying a Clinch Knot. Make six turns for material less than 8-pound test, five turns for material from 8- to 12-pound, and four turns for material up to 40-pound. (Use a Homer Rhode Loop for heavier material.)

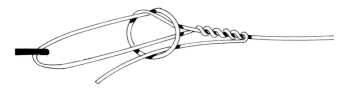

4. Pass the tag end back through the original overhand knot one final time. Again, it must enter the loop on the same side you have been using.

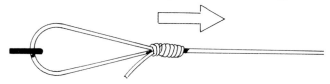

5. Tighten the knot by first pulling on the tag end until the turns tighten against the overhand. Next pull tightly on the fly and the standing part of the leader to finish the knot. Trim the tag end.

The Haywire Twist

1. Pass the wire through the hook eye and bend it back towards the standing part of the wire. Twist

the tag end around the standing part of the wire
five times.

2. Now make five barrel coils around the standing
   part of the wire, close together and at 90 degrees
   to the standing part.

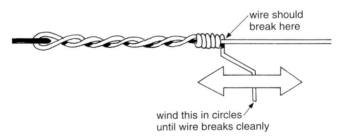

wire should
break here

wind this in circles
until wire breaks cleanly

3. Make a handle by bending the tag end of the wire
   at two places. Crank this handle back and forth
   until the wire breaks. Never cut the end of a Haywire Twist; the sharp end of the wire can be extremely dangerous.
4. Now make another Haywire Twist in the other
   end of the wire and attach the tippet to this second loop.

GLOSSARY

Backing: Thin, inexpensive, flexible line wound on the fly reel first, usually in lengths of 100 yards or more. Usually made of dacron or gel spun polyester. A fly line is about 100 feet long and a tippet about 9 feet. Some saltwater fish and salmon can run 200 yards before an angler can stop them. Backing provides insurance against a long screaming run.

Braided leader: A leader whose butt section is made from many tiny nylon filaments. The tapered butt section is more flexible than any other type and provides good turnover and delicate delivery. Tippets are of standard monofilament.

Butt section: The heaviest part of a leader, usually with a loop on the heavy end to facilitate easy connection to the fly line.

Class tippet: A tippet, usually doubled at both ends with a Bimini Twist, that is looped between the butt section and shock tippet of a saltwater leader. In order to be eligible for the IGFA record books, a class tippet must be at least 15 inches long and must test at a maximum of 2, 4, 6, 8, 12, 16, or 20 pounds, depending upon the line class in which the record is to be entered.

Compound taper: A taper that does not decrease at a steady rate. In a leader this refers to a taper with a relatively level butt section, followed by a quick taper, followed by a long, level tippet section.

Copolymer: A mixture of two different polymers of the same organic compound. In tippet material this is usually a mixture of nylon polymers.

Drag: 1. Mechanical tension, usually adjustable, on a fly reel's outgoing line to help tire a fish. 2. Movement of a fly contrary to a stream's currents that looks unnatural to a fish.

Fluorocarbon: Polyviylidenfluoride (PDVF), a plastic developed for the packaging industry. It is strong, clear, and resistant to degradation by ultraviolet light and solvents. In fishing lines, it is more abrasion-resistant than nylon. It is also less visible and than nylon under water and sinks quicker. It was first used for fly-fishing leaders in the mid-1990s.

Gut leader: Prior to World War II, fly leaders and tippets were made from drawn silkworm gut. It was relatively weak and had to be soaked well before use; it was quickly replaced by nylon.

IGFA: The International Game Fish Association. This organization is considered by most anglers to be the official record-keeper of fly-fishing and conventional tackle rod-and-reel records. The IGFA sets rules for tackle and procedures for becoming eligible for world records and has an extensive testing lab for analyzing leaders used to catch record fish. (Leaders must be sent to the IGFA when applying for a world record.)

Index of refraction: A measure of how much a clear material will bend or refract light rays.

Knotless leader: A machine-made leader that has been extruded from a machine to make a long, thin taper.

Knotted leader: A leader tapered by joining level sections of different diameters of tippet material with knots.

Leader: A thin, flexible connection between the heavy, opaque fly line and the fly.

Monofilament: A clear, flexible filament (a single strand) in fishing lines made from nylon or PVDF.

Nylon: A plastic developed in the mid-twentieth century to replace silk, in particular for stockings and parachutes. It is now a ubiquitous part of our lives and comes in many different formulas. A copolymer of nylon 6 and nylon 66 is commonly used in leader and tippet material.

Poly leader: A leader whose butt section is made from a clear, floating, tapered polyethylene section. These leaders straighten easily and will unfurl a long tippet with ease. Tippets are of standard monofilament.

PVDF: See fluorocarbon.

Shock tippet: A heavy piece of monofilament or wire that allows a large fish to be caught on a relatively light class tippet. The shock tippet absorbs a heavy strike, but its main purpose is to keep the lighter class tippet from being chewed or cut by a fish's sharp body parts.

Specific gravity: A compound's weight in relation to water. The higher the number above 1.0, the faster the material will sink.

Tippet: The thinnest part of a leader; the part that attaches to the fly. The tippet can be a separate piece of material, or a relative term that indicates the thinner end of a knotless leader.

Transition piece: The middle sections of a leader, in between the butt and tippet sections.

X-sizes: The diameters of leader materials are given X-sizes that refer to the material's diameter. These sizes came from the old gut-leader designations, but are still used because they are easier to remember than thousandths of inches.

THE ORVIS KNOTTED LEADER FORMULAS

7½-Foot Leaders

0X		1X	
LENGTH OF SECTION IN INCHES	**DIAMETER OF SECTION IN INCHES**	**LENGTH OF SECTION IN INCHES**	**DIAMETER OF SECTION IN INCHES**
24	.019	24	.019
16	.017	16	.017
14	.015	14	.015
9	.013	9	.013
9	.012	9	.011
18	.011	18	.010

2X		3X	
LENGTH OF SECTION IN INCHES	**DIAMETER OF SECTION IN INCHES**	**LENGTH OF SECTION IN INCHES**	**DIAMETER OF SECTION IN INCHES**
24	.019	24	.019
16	.017	16	.017
14	.015	14	.015
9	.013	6	.013
9	.011	6	.011
18	.009	18	.008

4X

LENGTH OF SECTION IN INCHES	DIAMETER OF SECTION IN INCHES
24	.019
16	.017
14	.015
6	.013
6	.011
18	.008

9-Foot Leaders

0X

LENGTH OF SECTION IN INCHES	DIAMETER OF SECTION IN INCHES
36	.021
16	.019
12	.017
8	.015
8	.013
8	.012
20	.011

1X

LENGTH OF SECTION IN INCHES	DIAMETER OF SECTION IN INCHES
36	.021
16	.019
12	.017
8	.015
8	.013
8	.012
20	.010

2X

LENGTH OF SECTION IN INCHES	DIAMETER OF SECTION IN INCHES
36	.021
16	.019
12	.017
8	.015
8	.013
8	.011
20	.009

3X

LENGTH OF SECTION IN INCHES	DIAMETER OF SECTION IN INCHES
36	.021
16	.019
12	.017
6	.015
6	.013
6	.011
6	.009
20	.008

4X

LENGTH OF SECTION IN INCHES	DIAMETER OF SECTION IN INCHES
36	.021
16	.019
12	.017
6	.015
6	.013
6	.011
6	.009
20	.007

5X

LENGTH OF SECTION IN INCHES	DIAMETER OF SECTION IN INCHES
28	.021
14	.019
12	.017
10	.015
6	.013
6	.011
6	.009
6	.007
20	.006

12-Foot Leaders

4X

LENGTH OF SECTION IN INCHES	DIAMETER OF SECTION IN INCHES
36	.021
24	.019
16	.017
12	.015
7	.013
7	.011
7	.009
7	.008
28	.007

5X

LENGTH OF SECTION IN INCHES	DIAMETER OF SECTION IN INCHES
36	.021
24	.019
16	.017
12	.015
7	.013
7	.011
7	.009
7	.008
28	.006

6X

LENGTH OF SECTION IN INCHES	DIAMETER OF SECTION IN INCHES
36	.021
24	.019
16	.017
12	.015
7	.013
7	.011
7	.009
7	.007
28	.005

7X

LENGTH OF SECTION IN INCHES	DIAMETER OF SECTION IN INCHES
28	.021
18	.019
16	.017
14	.015
12	.013
7	.011
7	.009
7	.007
7	.005
28	.004

INDEX